THE MIAMI RIVER

AND ITS TRIBUTARIES

BY DONALD C. GABY

THE HISTORICAL ASSOCIATION OF SOUTHERN FLORIDA
MIAMI

THE MIAMI RIVER

The pictures on the covers are turn-of-the-century photochrom prints produced by the Detroit Photo Company. Both the front and back covers depict the mouth of the Miami River with the Royal Palm Hotel most notable on the north bank, circa 1898. From the collection of the Historical Association of Southern Florida.

The Historical Association of Southern Florida
101 West Flagler Street, Miami, Florida 33130

Library of Congress Catalog Number: 93-079393

ISBN: 0-935761-04-7

This book was produced with the generous support
of the following sponsors working with the
Historical Association of Southern Florida:

Merrill-Stevens Dry Dock Co.

Florida Marine Towing Co., Inc.

Biscayne Bay Pilots Association

Miami River Marine Group

Teo A. Babun, Jr.

Walter R. Ferguson

Dedicated to those brave pioneers
of the 19th century who loved the river
enough to endure the hardships
before there was a city.

Table of Contents

List of Illustrations

Acknowledgements

The author wishes to acknowledge his debt and gratitude to three special ladies. He is especially indebted and grateful to historian Arva Moore Parks McCabe, M.A., who encouraged and guided his first attempt at historical research almost two decades ago. Arva continued to provide encouragement and guidance, willingly shared much of her own material on the Miami River, and set a high standard for scholarship and good writing. He is indebted and grateful to historian Thelma Peters, Ph.D., for her inspiration, introductions to older Miamians who knew the river, and the gift of two books and several photographs that might otherwise have been overlooked. Last but not least, he is grateful to his wife, Elouise, for her patience and understanding over many years of effort. She also read each chapter for coherence, clarity and typographical errors.

He is deeply grateful to those many unnamed individuals with special knowledge of the river—some of them very busy individuals—who gladly shared their knowledge with him.

He thanks the Historical Museum of Southern Florida for its support in the publication of this book, and especially the following staff members: Natalie Brown for her editing, layout and valuable suggestions to improve the text, Dawn Hugh for assistance in finding photographs and other material in the Research Center, Sam Joseph for the tedious task of optically scanning the original text and creating the initial layout and George Chillag for assistance with illustration selection and photography. The author also thanks Sam Boldrick of the Florida Room, Metro-Dade Public Library, for his willing assistance in locating information and for the use of certain materials.

He thanks the Seaport Map Co., in particular Richard Troutner, for the free use of their excellent maps of the Miami River system and environs which form the base for the map of the river on the inside back cover.

The author is entirely responsible for any errors of fact or misstatements, and any omissions. He sincerely requests that better informed readers let him know of such things. Any opinions expressed are entirely those of the author.

Introduction

This book is based on the author's ongoing research on the history of the Miami River and its tributaries. It is not a comprehensive history of the river, but rather a collection of information gathered during some seven years of research and interviews. A great deal of information was also obtained from reading early Miami newspapers and takes the reader into the late 1930s. Accordingly, certain sites or activities are treated in some depth while others may be inadequately treated or omitted entirely.

The author's earlier work published in 1990, *An Historical Guide to the Miami River and Its Tributarties,* was designed as a pocket guide for persons going up (or down) the river by boat, or following the river along its land borders. This larger work reflects in part the additional knowledge acquired since that earlier effort. It contains three new chapters. The first of these, *The Natural Miami River,* attempts to describe the river prior to any significant changes brought about by humans. Reference was made to the earliest known surveys and descriptions. The second new chapter, *Man-Made Changes to the River,* describes the major physical changes to the river since the founding of the City of Miami and the increased human presence. A third new chapter, *Pollution,* is included as it is a matter of much concern at the present while relatively few people are aware of the history *and progress* made.

Those readers not interested in these preliminary chapters may skip directly to Chapter 4 to begin a journey up the river.

A Select Bibliography has been added for readers desiring more specific knowledge or authority, plus an *Index* for convenience.

As in the earlier guide, basic geographical reference is to the various streets and avenues that cross the river, or to other prominent features. (See the map on the inside back cover.) The bridges are further identified by color, following the "Rainbow Plan" sponsored in 1985 by the Miami River Coordinating Committee to improve the aesthetic appeal of the river and its environs. (The bridges are painted as routine maintenance is performed.)

The text is arranged for a person making a journey from Biscayne Bay up the Miami River to its headwaters, then on the Miami Canal to the end of navigation. Side trips up the various tributaries, both natural and artificial, to the salinity dams or other obstructions to navigation are included throughout the journey. Most chapters include a section between two bridges. Whether so bounded or not, the description usually will proceed upstream along the north shore first, then along the south shore, ending with a paragraph or more on the upstream bridge where appropriate. In that way, readers interested in a particular site can easily find it. The term "river" will often be used here to mean the entire complex of natural and artificial waterways.

The length of chapters was dictated by the amount of history to relate, or simply by the degree of the author's knowledge about some sections and earlier periods. The author's research has taken him to the National Archives, Library of Congress, Defense Department Library, Florida State Archives, Florida Department of Natural Resources, Dade County Public Records Library,

Historical Museum of Southern Florida Research Center, Miami-Dade Public Library and university and public libraries. Fact gathering from early Miami newspapers from 1896 to 1938 has taken seven years. Preparation of the manuscript was essentially complete by early August 1992. Only changes required by the passage of Hurricane Andrew were made later. The author hopes that a second edition in the future will carry on the quest to tell the Miami River history to the present.

The author invites knowledgeable readers to inform him of any errors noted, and significant river history that might be included in a future edition.

P.O. Box 45-1337
Miami, FL 33245

Chapter 1
The Natural Miami River

Juan Ponce de Leon probably was the first European to set eyes on the Miami River of Florida. When he discovered Biscayne Bay in July 1513, he appears to have visited the mouth of the river because he noted the large Tequesta Indian village there on the north shore. At the very edge of the bay just north of the river's mouth was a very large Indian midden or burial mound. Some 100 feet long by 75 feet wide, this mound stood 20 to 25 feet above sea level and was one of the highest points along that stretch of the coast. (With tall trees growing on the mound, it served as a landmark for sailors passing along that coast for centuries afterward.) Besides those attractions, Ponce de Leon must also have needed fresh water, of which there was an abundance in the spring-fed river.

The name "Miami" is said to come from an Indian word meaning "sweet water." During the 18th and 19th centuries, the Miami River was also known as the "Garbrand River" (1765-71), "Rio Ratones" (1770-75), "Fresh Water River" (1799-1803), "Sweetwater River" (1808), and "Lemon River" (1823). During the Seminole Wars (1835-58) it was known as the Miami River and that name has lasted into the 20th century.

Visitors in the 19th century described the Miami River as the principal stream along the lower east coast of Florida and as a stream of rare beauty. It served the native Tequesta Indians for

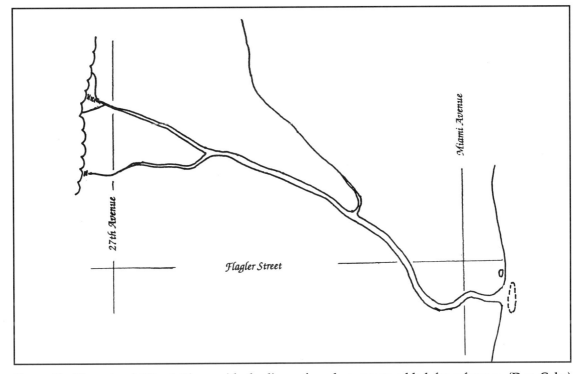

Figure 1A. The natural Miami River, with the lines of modern streets added for reference. (Don Gaby)

centuries before and after the arrival of the Spanish, and it served the Seminoles and others after Florida became a United States Territory in 1821. The river forked about three miles above its mouth at Biscayne Bay, and the larger north fork of the river, the main stream, terminated in a famous rapids or "falls" at its source only one mile farther on. The south fork also had a rapids, but it was a much smaller stream with much less of a fall at its source. Both forks of the river had their headwaters at the eastern edge of the Everglades, approximately four miles from Biscayne Bay.

During those early years and into the 20th century, persons entering the Everglades customarily did so on the south fork where there was less current and a shallow rapids falling less than a foot. Persons coming from the Everglades to Miami—or Fort Dallas as it was known during the Seminole Wars and afterward—normally used the north fork, either shooting the rapids or going around them to join the main stream of the river. Here the water fell about six feet while traversing some 450 feet of rapids. The flow over these rapids could be torrential, especially during the rainy season, and the north fork normally provided a swift current—the exceptions being during periods of extreme drought. At such times, the rapids might be completely dry or with little flow.

Some say that the Miami River is the shortest in the United States, or at least the shortest commercial river in the country. Although only four miles long from its source at the edge of the Everglades to its mouth at Biscayne Bay, it had a considerable fall before the Everglades were drained. Surveyor F. H. Geddes, by request of the Secretary of the Treasury, in 1849 ran a line of levels from the Everglades above the rapids to mean low water in the bay. (Even then draining the Everglades was being considered!) Geddes measured a drop of 6 feet 2.5 inches. At the time of measurement, the level of water in the "glades" was stated to be lower and the "tide in the bay" higher than ordinary, making this a conservative measurement. Geddes determined the average fall to be about 20 inches per mile. That was several times greater than the average fall per mile of the Ohio and Mississippi Rivers from Pittsburgh to the Gulf of Mexico.

About one and a half miles above the mouth of the river was a major tributary running to the north and northwest for about two miles. It took the name of "Wagner Creek" after William Wagner, an early pioneer who built his home by the creek in the late 1850s.

During the 19th century, that piece of land bounded by the north and south forks of the Miami River and by the Everglades to the west was often referred to as an "island" or as "Marshall's Island" after an early settler, George Marshall, who had his home on the north shore of the south fork. It surely must have seemed like an island, especially during the rainy summer season when the Everglades bounding it on the west stretched like an inland sea of grass and water as far as the eye could see, with an occasional tropical hardwood "hammock" island to add interest. ("Hammock" is from an Indian word meaning "shady place.")

Just below the rapids of the north fork was a lesser tributary that ran north a short distance. The author calls this "Ferguson Creek" after Thomas and George Ferguson, two brothers who settled there beside the creek and built a water-powered saw and coontie mill over it in 1845. Just downstream from Ferguson Creek a smaller tributary ran southwest, but it has been filled and can not be found today.

Water from the Everglades spilling over the coastal ridge and a multitude of fresh water springs fed the Miami River. The Everglades water had a darkish cast because of decaying vegetation from its source, but the spring water was perfectly clear. A scientist writing in 1896 described a huge spring which had its issue from one bank of the north fork just below the rapids where, during periods of low water, one could see the clear water from the spring mixing with the darkish water from the 'Glades. There were numerous subterranean springs below the river in addition to others along the shore. A very large spring, perhaps the mouth of a subterranean stream, issued from the river bottom in about 13 feet depth at today's Miami Avenue. Above the rapids of the north fork was a large spring-fed pool, about 10 feet deep and 75 feet across, from which the City of Miami initially drew its water. Here the water was very soft and said to gush above the surface of the spring. It measured 7° F colder (68° F in July) than the river or other nearby springs.

(A very narrow stream led into this pool from the west, and its source might be considered the river's headwaters. But there is some evidence that it was one of several such very small streams used by the Indians as "canoe trails" that were often not distinguishable. That small stream is shown on the map at the end of this book.)

There was a wide variety of vegetation. Along the western shore of Biscayne Bay once stood magnificent stands of red mangroves, and red mangroves also grew along the Miami River at least as far upstream as today's Fifth Street bridge, even to the fork. An oolitic limestone ridge ran along the shore of the bay and was cut by the river itself, that ridge being much higher in elevation toward the south. A high oolitic limestone ridge ran along the south shore of the river from about today's 11th to 19th Avenues with a low place near 16th Avenue. On such high ground, and often in other places, plants and large trees grew typical of southeast Florida's tropical hardwood hammocks—the live oak, gumbo limbo, mahogany, etc. Caribbean pines together with palmetto and the plant called "coontie" (*Zamia pumila*) covered other well drained ground, not so high as the ridges. Broad prairies of fertile soil were back from the river but occasionally reaching the shore, such as the Allapattah Prairie to the north of the river and to the west of Wagner Creek. In other places along the river, the shores were quite low and often marshy, sometimes sawgrass mud flats—good breeding grounds for mosquitoes. The point cradled by the forks of the river was a muddy flat. Bald cypress grew near the headwaters of both the north and south forks, and near the headwaters of Wagner and Ferguson Creeks. In other places one might find the pond apple, bays and willows. Coconut palms grew on the Miami River in the 1820s and were well established at the mouth of the river in the 1870s. (Perhaps the Spanish introduced them originally or a hurricane brought them to these shores, since they are not indigenous to the area.)

The river bottom was mostly rock with sandy places and occasional mud holes. A variety of multi-colored grasses and other aquatic plants covered the bottom, undulating back and forth in the swift current. Although fed by fresh water from the Everglades and from numerous springs, tidal action extended all the way to the headwaters. Several early reports note the tide rising and salt water from the sea as far upstream as the fork, and at least one report noted salt water at the rapids. As today, the denser salt water probably lay below the fresh. During times of drought the river sometimes turned brackish. The daily rise and fall of the water due to the astronomical tides was about two feet at the mouth of the river and often more depending on the season and phase of the moon. There was a great variety of salt water fishes, crabs, turtles, alligators and manatees. Some said the manatees even penetrated the Everglades.

Figure IB. The mouth of the Miami River as seen from Gilbert's wharf on the south bank east of today's Miami Avenue, ca. 1884. (Munroe Collection, Historical Museum of Southern Florida)

The original Miami River is barely recognizable today. It was short, but its dimensions were substantial. Offshore from the mouth was a sand bar with only a few feet of water above, blocking the entry of deeper draft vessels. The mouth of the river opened gently toward the northeast. It was about 300 feet wide and eight to 13 feet deep, with steep banks on both sides. From today's Brickell Avenue to Miami Avenue the river was from 320 to 345 feet wide and from seven to 14 feet deep. Down the center below today's Miami Avenue was a narrow rock shelf with only about seven feet of water. About half the width of the river at the upstream end, it tapered to a point downstream near the line of today's Southeast 1st Avenue. From above today's Miami Avenue to near today's N.W. 3rd Street, the river's width varied from 230 to 280 feet with depths from five to 11 feet. Above this point it gradually narrowed to only 130 feet wide at today's Fifth Street bridge with depths from five to 10 feet.

Just above the Fifth Street bridge, Wagner Creek led off to the north, then northwest. The creek was about 20-25 feet wide where it joined the river and substantially the same to about 11th Street, after which it tapered down gradually for the remaining mile of its length.

Although the mouth of the river opened toward the northeast, the river soon turned gently to just north of west, then southwest with a broad bend marking its southernmost position between today's Metrorail and S.W. 2nd Avenue bridges. From there, it ran generally northwest to Wagner Creek.

Above Wagner Creek the river widened again, being 150 to 200 feet wide between about today's 9th and 13th Avenues with depths of five to nine feet. Near today's 14th and 16th Avenues was a "shallows," where the river became 250 to 275 feet wide and only three to six feet deep.

Figure lC. Miccosukee Indians on the Miami River, ca. 1914. Compare the traditional Indian headdress on one man with the modern hat on the other. (Curt Teich Postcard Archives)

Here the current ran more swiftly because of the shallow depth, and much of the bottom was rocky. From these shallows to today's 17th Avenue the river tapered down to about 160 feet wide, with depths of seven feet or more. It was wider above 17th Avenue, reaching about 220 feet, then tapered down to 160 feet again at the fork. It made a double bend just below the fork, still unchanged.

From the fork near today's l9th Avenue, the south fork of the river ran southwest a short distance and then generally west to the edge of the Everglades. This south fork, more like a tributary and once known as "Marshall's Creek" or "Wilson's Creek," was about 80 feet wide at its mouth but narrowed rapidly to about 60 feet, then tapered down to about 20 feet wide where it joined the Everglades.

The north fork of the river, always the main stream, ran generally west-northwest to the edge of the Everglades. It was about 185 feet wide at its mouth—wider than the river just below the fork and more than twice as wide as the south fork. It tapered down to about 80 feet wide at today's Miami Canal entrance near 24th Court, to 35 feet wide at 27th Avenue, and to about 25 feet wide at the foot of the rapids near today's 29th Avenue. Here it had rocky banks. It was six to 10 feet deep over much of its length, and at least three to four feet deep just below the rapids. The actual depth at any particular time naturally depended upon the stage of the tide and input of fresh water.

The rapids of the north fork of the Miami River are considered to be the headwaters of the river. However, as noted previously, there was a large spring-fed pool above the rapids which was fed also by at least one narrow stream running into it from the west (see the map). Also, it should be noted that the geologic structure of the rapids is yet undisturbed—these rapids were never

Figure 1D. The rapids of the north fork of the Miami River, ca. 1896. (Munroe Collection, Historical Museum of Southern Florida)

dynamited—and that only the old north fork of the river above about 26th Avenue has never been dredged.

Until the coming of the railroad and the founding of Miami in 1896, there were no man-made changes to the natural river. Several pioneer families had homes along the river. But they built simple wharfs or boat landings without significantly altering the river itself. One could sail a small boat well beyond the fork with a following breeze, and the trip back down was usually aided by a swift current.

Originally, and for more than a decade after the founding of the City of Miami in 1896, the Miami River was almost everywhere a beautifully clear stream. Until the start of the Miami Canal in 1909, it appears that there were few enough people and a sufficiently abundant flow of water that the river could maintain its clean condition most of the time. There was some dredging and filling of the downstream portion of the river and on the south fork during that period. Major changes followed opening of the Miami Canal in 1912. Destruction of the natural river was almost complete with the deepening and widening of the Miami River and Canal by the Army Corps of Engineers in 1932-33. Few today remember the river before that final event.

Chapter 2
Man-Made* Changes to the River

This account will progress upstream from Biscayne Bay so readers may easily locate an area of interest. It will end with a summary of the major man-made changes in chronological order.

The first reported effort to improve navigation into the Miami River came from a newspaper account. It states that in 1856, during the Third Seminole War, the Army began cutting a channel through the sandbar just off the mouth of the river in order to facilitate the landing of military supplies stored on Key Biscayne and brought to Fort Dallas. A decision by the War Department not to make Fort Dallas a permanent post led to abandonment of that effort. That such a channel would have been useful is without doubt.

In 1896, Henry Flagler dug a nine-foot deep channel from the mouth of the Miami River into deeper water in Biscayne Bay on a route around Cape Florida. At the same time, he removed

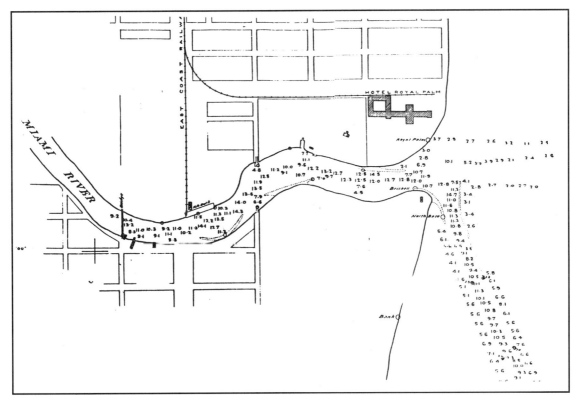

Figure 2A. An adaptation of Lt. Col. W. H. H. Benyaurd's map of the Mouth of the Miami River from a survey made during October and November 1896, U.S. Engineer Office, St. Augustine, Florida, January 1897. (P. K. Yonge Library, University of Florida)

*The use of the term "man-made" is recognized by the publisher and author to be gender-biased and perhaps somewhat inaccurate in this context as women very likely also made changes to the river throughout its history. However, the author has chosen this terminology for its communicative accuracy.

many shallow areas in the river below his Florida East Coast Railway terminal dock near today's S.W. First Avenue, making a channel 60 feet wide. And he widened the river slightly just below the terminal dock landing to accommodate the sidewheel steamer *City of Richmond* which was 225 feet in length, 50 feet in beam, drawing 7-1/2 feet.

The U.S. Army Corps of Engineers surveyed this channel and the lower Miami River at the time of this work. (A survey by the Corps in 1899-1900 concluded that a ship channel to the ocean via Cape Florida would not be feasible for more than 12 feet of depth.)

In January 1907, Flagler interests completed enlarging the marina of the Royal Palm Hotel on the north side of the river near its mouth. The marina initially consisted of just one long pier extending into the river at a slight angle to the shoreline. The new marina had three short piers extending into the river at an acute angle with the natural shoreline, running out from where they filled a considerable portion of the north side of the river west of the the new piers, creating a new shoreline. This work reduced the width of the mouth of the river from about 300 feet to only 205 feet. It is perhaps the only instance where the natural river's width was significantly decreased by human intervention.

The Florida East Coast Hotel Co. built a larger marina for the Royal Palm Hotel in 1924 at the south end of today's Miami Center property. Its construction was on landfill taken from the adjacent bay bottom during 1922-24 in conjunction with the building of Bayfront Park during 1924-25. These were major projects that greatly extended the natural shoreline of the bay immediately north of the mouth of the river and permanently altered the configuration of the shoreline where previously the mouth of the river had opened gently toward the northeast. The new marina consisted of 10 short piers running out from the shoreline and one long pier parallel to the navigation channel, abutting the older three-pier marina then filled in to the west. This construction further restricted the entrance to the river. This marina lasted through World War II, after which it was filled. Today, the riverwalk south of the Intercontinental Hotel which is along the north side of the river at its mouth follows the line of the long pier of the former marina.

We should note that from the earliest development of the City of Miami, private citizens, both residents and business people, freely dug boat slips and altered the shorelines by a great deal of filling and cutting. Permits for such work were not required. Much of the filling was to remove low areas where mosquitoes were known to breed. These changes are too numerous to note and individually not large, but taken together they constitute major alterations to both shores for much of the river's length, especially in the downtown area. (In 1916, the shoreline southward from Brickell Point was straightened and filled, but that did not affect the Miami River itself.)

After Miami Canal's opening in March 1912 — that state project began in 1909 from the river near N.W. 24th Court — a massive flow of water from the Everglades lasted for three weeks as the water levels there dropped. The flow then continued less vigorously. Sediment from the canal, consisting of Everglades muck and finely ground stone from the dredging, silted the downstream portions of the river sufficiently to block the entry of large commercial vessels. The lower portion of the river was dredged to remove this silt in August 1912, then again in 1913 and 1914. Much of this material went to fill parts of the river's borders, plus Brickell Point, and to start a spoil island just off the mouth of the river south of the navigation channel. (Chapter 4 describes this island now known as Claughton Island.)

Figure 2B. Dredge on the Miami Canal, ca. 1911. (Matlack Collection, Historical Museum of Southern Florida)

The natural river included a rock ledge that was about half the width of the river just below Miami Avenue and tapered to a point at S.E. First Avenue. During September and October 1912, the city removed this rock ledge almost completely to provide a total of 11 feet of water across the river. Only a small portion at the downstream end was left.

The Miami Steamship Co. filled a triangular portion of the river on the north shore immediately east of Miami Avenue around 1913 to provide a longer dock for its ships. On the opposite side of Miami Avenue, Flagler originally excavated a portion of the north shore to accomodate large vessels. That cut was modified by 1918, and filled again after World War II.

John Seybold straightened and deepened the lower portion of Wagner Creek to make his Seybold Canal in 1918. The Seybold Canal ran directly north from the river along N.W. 7th Avenue to about 8th Street, where it turned northwest and ended in a turning basin just below 11th Street. From there to 20th Street, Wagner Creek was later channelized where it passes through Highland Park and today's Civic Center, being covered or filled above 20th Street to 17th Avenue.

The shallow portion of the natural river between about 14th and 16th Avenues appears to have been removed around 1921 in conjunction with the widening and deepening of the Miami Canal from the Miami River to its junction with the South New River Canal. This was because the drainage engineers thought it useless to enlarge that portion of the Miami Canal for drainage unless obstructions in the river were also removed to allow a freer flow of water. (As early as 1909 a portion of these "shallows" may have been removed in order to pass the dredge that began excavation of the Miami Canal.)

In 1916, B. B. Tatum "leveled" the shoreline of what would become the Grove Park subdivision by removing some of the river bottom and adjacent south shore immediately downstream from 17th Avenue—in that way making the river wider below 17th Avenue than it was above it.

W. A. Williams excavated the Lawrence Park Canal to join the Miami River from the south, just west of N.W. 17th Avenue, during 1921-22. It includes a turning basin at its head near N.W. 7th Street and has a short branch canal running west near Ninth Street. This project was unique on the river in that it cut through an oolitic limestone ridge 12 feet high that ran along the south shore in that area.

The shallow rapids at the headwaters of the south fork of the Miami River (near N.W. 29th Avenue) were blasted out in 1908 in connection with the construction of the Huyler-Comfort Canal, known today simply as the Comfort Canal. The canal begins near the salinity dam just west of 27th Avenue. The south fork of the river was deepened and widened in some places about that time. Fern Isle, an islet in the stream above 22nd Avenue created in the 1920s while dredging a new channel, was later removed, leaving the south fork wider in that area.

Hugh Martin and a group of the adjacent property owners dredged the old north fork of the river about eight feet deep from the entrance to the Miami Canal at 24th Court upstream to near 26th Avenue during the late 1950s. (Beyond this point to the former rapids is the only stretch of the river never dredged.)

Figure 2C. The dredge *Governor Herrick* **of the Bowers-Southern Dredging Co. (Historical Museum of Southern Florida)**

The State of Florida began construction in May 1909 of the Miami Canal, running west-northwest from the river at about today's N.W. 24th Court. This was part of the great Everglades drainage project begun during the administration of Governor Napolean B. Broward. The initial specifications for the Miami Canal were for a width of 60 feet and depth of 8 feet, running all the way to Lake Okeechobee. The dredge *Miami*, built especially for this project, began the excavation. In the spring of 1910, an earthen dam was installed in the canal to contain sufficient water to float the dredge. A permanent boat lock and dam near today's 34th Avenue replaced it in late 1912. After completing only a little more than four miles of the canal by July 1910, the state contracted the job to the Furst-Clark Construction Co. The Miami Canal opened in March 1912, but its completion all the way to Lake Okeechobee took until April 1913. Although a depth of 8 feet was specified, along much of the route only the easy-to-remove muck was taken out, leaving long shallow stretches with a hard rock bottom.

During 1917 to 1923, the state contracted the Bowers-Southern Dredging Co. to deepen the Miami Canal to 12 feet and make it 90 feet wide from its junction with the Miami River at 24th Court to just above its junction with the South New River Canal.

Construction of the Tamiami Canal began in 1916 to provide fill for the Tamiami Trail highway across the Everglades then being built. In 1919, a canal to join it with the Miami Canal near 30th Avenue was authorized. Many during the 1920s knew that connecting canal as the "Cross-cut Canal" or as the "Comfort Canal" (because that canal joined it near today's Blue Lagoon Lake south of Miami International Airport). Today, the Tamiami Canal begins at the Miami Canal and the old names are mostly forgotten.

Palmer Lake, off the Miami Canal near 25th Street, is entirely artificial. Excavation began in the early 1920s and was mostly accomplished before the 1926 hurricane.

An effort to deepen and widen the Miami River began in late 1927. Congressman W. J. Sears asked the Army Corps of Engineers to provide a channel 16 feet deep to Miami Avenue, then 10 feet deep or more for three to four miles above the bay, that is, to about 27th Avenue. In early 1930, Miami Mayor Reeder led a delegation in testimony before the Congress, arguing the need for flood control. They requested a channel 150 feet wide, 15 feet deep, and nine miles long; that is, from Biscayne Bay to well beyond today's Palmetto Expressway! Representative Ruth Bryan Owen—the first woman elected to Congress from Florida and a resident of Coral Gables—led this effort. It was for both navigation and flood control, part of the argument being to protect Miami's airport from flooding. This resulted in approval by the Rivers and Harbors Committee of $800,000 for this river work. However, President Hoover threatened a veto if the total cost of the nation-wide bill was excessive. Fortunately, the Senate agreed on the amount for the Miami River and the president signed the bill into law.

This Act of Congress on 3 July 1930 authorized a project for deepening and widening the Miami River and the Miami Canal from Biscayne Bay to about 35th Street. The appropriation was for $800,000—equivalent to about $13,600,000 in 1990 dollars. That project provided for a navigation channel 150 feet wide and 15 feet deep for a distance of 3 miles above the mouth of the river (about to the fork at 19th Avenue), thence 125 feet wide and 15 feet deep to a point 4-1/8th miles above the mouth (to the Tamiami Canal entrance), thence 90 feet wide and 15 feet deep to a point

5-1/2 miles above the mouth (to just below 35th Street). It was considerably less distance than originally hoped, but considered quite satisfactory by all concerned parties.

The Congress adjourned before the appropriation bill was authorized, and it looked as if the project was on hold until the next session. In December 1930, an emergency appropriation provided funds for Miami's Harbor, but not for the Miami River, because local interests were not cooperating with certain requirements. Almost another year would be wasted.

The act authorizing this improvement stipulated that no expense would be incurred by the United States for acquiring any lands needed for the purpose of the improvement, and that local interests would provide all needed spoil-disposal areas. The start of the project was delayed some 17 months until the City of Miami complied with those requirements. Part of the problem was that there was little room for the spoil along the river's banks below the Fifth Street bridge. Finally, by a Resolution of 19 November 1931, the City Commission guaranteed: 1) that all lands required for right-of-way and spoil areas for this project would be furnished without cost to the United States; and 2) that the City of Miami would hold and save the United States free of all claims for damages to structures or otherwise due to the execution of the work.

Prior to the start of this work, the city strengthened the foundations of five older bridges. The city had to decide between building longer bridge spans to cross the wider navigation channel—at great expense—or accepting a more narrow channel at the bridges and strengthening some of them. City officials believed that the deeper channel would bring a greater flow of water and increase the strain on the river bridges. The bridges strengthened were at Miami Avenue, S.W. 2nd

Figure 2D. The dredge *Norman H. Davis* with 1,000 horsepower, cutter and suction, was able to force a 20-inch stream of water a full mile. (Historical Museum of Southern Florida)

Avenue, Flagler Street, N.W. 5th Street and 27th Avenue. (The bridge at 27th Avenue was included even though it was technically outside the city limits.)

The U.S. Army Corps of Engineers contracted the project to the Standard Dredging Co. of New York. That firm subcontracted the bulk of the job to the Clark Dredging Co. of Miami. The subcontractor began the excavation from the upstream end near 35th Street using the dredge *Arundel* in March 1932. About the same time the Webster Construction Co., another subcontractor, began clearing the river bottom of obstructions, including the remains of Miami Lock No. 1 on the Miami Canal. Later, the prime contractor began excavating from the mouth of the river. They planned to meet at the 5th Street bridge. Unable to handle the downstream end of the job either, the Standard company subcontracted that portion also to Clark Dredging. Clark used the giant dredge *Norman H. Davis* from the mouth of the river.

An early problem was where to put the spoil, especially that taken out below the 5th Street bridge (the downtown portion of the river). For a while in 1931, three large spoil islands were proposed well east of Bayfront Park and south of the County (today's MacArthur) Causeway. Hotel owners and other citizens objected to placing it there in the bay well east of Bayfront Park, especially when spoil promised to remain out-of-sight below the surface began to appear above it. The city gained authorization to bulkhead and fill Burlingame Island to about 21 acres. The project

Figure 2E. Aerial view of Burlingame Island and the Florida East Coast Hotel Co. property, 1940. The Brickell Avenue bridge is in the left half of this shot facing north. (Historical Museum of Southern Florida)

was 10.3 percent complete as of 30 June 1932. By April 1933, digging had progressed upstream to S.W. 2nd Avenue. The project was about 94 percent complete as of 30 June 1933. Indirect evidence suggests that the dredges met near 12th Avenue in August 1933. In many places the full 15 feet of depth was not achieved.

Late August 1933 saw completion of this project after 17-1/2 months of work. The dredging was accomplished for a total cost of $581,378.58; that is, about 73 percent of the funds appropriated, well under budget. Much of the spoil from the river was used to raise the elevation of lands adjacent to the river and canal.

Many river people still living say that this widening and deepening of the Miami River and Canal in the early 1930s destroyed the beautiful natural river and whatever wild character it then retained. Almost all of the natural vegetation along its shores was either removed or buried with spoil. One can gain an appreciation of the magnitude of the damage done by reference to Figure 2F. Looking eastward, this aerial photograph of the 27th Avenue bridge under construction in 1939 shows the old north fork of the river above (west of) 24th Court close to its natural width. Below (east of) its junction with the Miami Canal at 24th Court, the Miami River appears about three times as wide as it does above that junction.

Figure 2F. Aerial view of the N.W. 27th Avenue bridge on the Miami Canal under construction, looking eastward, 1939. Note the broad Miami Canal to the left, the narrow old north fork of the Miami River to the right foreground, and the artificially widened Miami River below its junction with the Miami Canal in the far upper right. (Historical Museum of Southern Florida)

Deepening and widening the Miami River and Canal in the early 1930s worsened the problem of salt water intrusion that began with excavation of the Miami and other canals early in this century. In 1945, a salinity control structure—a dam—was installed in the Miami Canal below 36th Street. In 1970, similar structures were installed in the Tamiami Canal below 42nd Avenue and in the Comfort Canal at 28th Avenue.

Chronological Summary of Major Man-Made Changes

1856	The U.S. Army cut a channel partly through the sandbar off the mouth of the Miami River.
1896	Henry Flagler dredged a channel nine feet deep from the mouth of the river into the deeper water of Biscayne Bay on a route to Cape Florida. He also removed shallow places in the river below the F.E.C. Railway terminal dock near S.W. 1st Avenue.
1907	Flagler enlarged the marina at the Royal Palm Hotel, filling in much of the north side of the river near its mouth, significantly reducing the width of the river at its entrance.
1908	The low rapids at the headwaters of the south fork of the river were removed in conjunction with dredging the Huyler-Comfort Canal. Other parts of the south fork were dredged about the same time.
1909-13	The State of Florida dredged the Miami Canal, running from the north shore of the river at about 24th Court.
1912	Sediment consisting of Everglades muck and finely ground rock from the newly opened Miami Canal that accumulated in the downstream portion of the river was removed and placed on adjacent low land and also used to start a spoil island off the mouth of the river.
1912	The City of Miami removed a rock ledge in the center of the river below Miami Avenue to provide 11 feet of water.
1917-23	The State of Florida deepened the Miami Canal.
1918	John Seybold straightened and deepened the lower portion of Wagner Creek to make the Seybold Canal.
1920	A "cross-cut" canal to join the Tamiami Canal to the Miami Canal was constructed.
1921	The shallow portion of the river near 14-16th Avenues was removed.
1921-22	W. A. Williams excavated the Lawrence Park Canal.
1922-24	The F.E.C. Hotel Co. enlarged the marina of the Royal Palm Hotel on land dredged from the adjacent bay bottom in conjunction with the construction of Bayfront Park, further restricting the entrance to the river.
1926	George Palmer completed the major excavation of Palmer Lake.
1932-33	The U.S. Army Corps of Engineers deepened and widened the Miami River and Canal from Biscayne Bay to about 35th Street.
1945	A salinity control dam was installed on the Miami Canal below 36th Street.
1950s	Private individuals deepened the old north fork between about 24th Court and 26th Avenue.
1970	Salinity control dams were installed on the Tamiami Canal and the south fork of the river where the Comfort Canal begins.

Chapter 3
Pollution

The Miami River ran clear and clean throughout its length until the founding of the City of Miami in 1896. Those few settlers who had their homes by or on the river did not alter the pristine condition of the water, natural processes being more than adequate to compensate for any human waste or other pollution.

The city got off to a bad start when Henry Flagler laid the first sanitary sewer down Avenue D (today's Miami Avenue) and right into the river. It connected with another sewer line along Fourteenth Street (today's S.E. 2nd Street) that served Flagler's Royal Palm Hotel. The sewer outlet into the river was just two blocks upstream from the grounds of the Royal Palm Hotel. Flagler did not do this without consideration. He consulted Dr. J. Y. Porter, first health officer of the State of Florida, who advised Flagler that such a sewer into the river would not be a problem for a city of 50,000 or fewer people, a count that Miami did not reach for several decades. January 1897 saw completion of that first sewer. In July 1902, believing that sewage disposal was properly a municipal responsibility, Flagler presented his sewerage system to the city. The city fathers gladly accepted the gift. Flagler paid to install that system and maintained it for six years at a cost of $12,000 to $13,000—equivalent to about one third of a million dollars in 1990.

By 1904, plans were being laid to improve the sewerage system to dump sewage "well down the bay." A bond issue in 1906 included provision for a sewer line into Biscayne Bay at today's S.E. 2nd Street. The filth emanating from these sewers soon became infamous.

Figure 3A. Laying Miami's first sanitary sewer line on Avenue D, today's Miami Avenue, and into the Miami River, 1896. (Historical Museum of Southern Florida)

The public's concern crested in June 1908 when the body of a baby girl floated out of the Avenue D (Miami Avenue) sewer outlet into the river. Men who regularly gathered there on the bridge to watch the fish feeding saw the infant rising to the surface with the excrement and refuse from the sewer. It was a white baby girl, five to six months old, and appeared to have died a natural death. By August, a group of citizens presented the City Council with a signed petition "humbly praying" that the Avenue D sewer into the river be rerouted into the bay where it would reach the "channel" (Flagler's old ship channel) and the sewage more easily carried into the bay. By August of the following year, the City Council responded to the problem by extending the Avenue D sewer further into the river, placing it deeper, and turning the outlet to point with the current—in that way assuring that the sewage would enter the bay before rising to the surface!

Author Van E. Huff noted the first obvious discoloration of the bay's waters in 1910. He wrote: "This was coincident with the initial excavation of the Miami Canal which began in May 1909 and continued until the spring of 1910 without any dam to contain dredged material suspended in the water. The dredge captain believed that there would be sufficient water flowing from the Everglades to float the dredge, but that proved not true and a temporary earthen dam was built . . . ." By the time that dam was built, more than four miles of canal had been dug and much of the material moved down the river to the bay. This was a slimy mess consisting of Everglades muck combined with finely ground rock from the dredging. The problem was no doubt a combination of that material with increased sewage from the city. When the Miami Canal opened in March 1912, there was a tremendous flow of muck and finely ground rock down the river and into the bay. Such accumulated sediment had to be removed several times from the downstream portion of the river. In the bay, it became difficult to find white sand because it was covered with muck.

The experience of the Royal Palm Hotel is interesting in this regard. From its beginning, the hotel filled its natatorium (swimming pool) with salt water pumped from the bay. In late 1912, they found that bay water pumped in was very murky. Indeed, an inch of sediment settled to the bottom of the pool. This caused them to drill a 58 foot deep well on the hotel grounds where in January 1913 they found fine salt water at 76-78° F temperature.

As the city grew, so did the number of sanitary sewers emptying into the Miami River and Biscayne Bay. By 1920, three sewers emptied into the bay and 10 into the river. That year, Dr. C. F. Saylor, president of the Board of Health, stated, "The city by dumping sewage into the river and bay, is committing a crime far worse than for which it is arresting persons."

On some days the foul odors from sewage floating in the river was wafted to homes two and three blocks away, and on hot days the odor was obvious to persons driving across the two bridges. Some feared that floating excrement left on the sides of the river banks when the tide went out would dry out and blow about the city. Again the city fathers planned a better system— screening, drying, and burning the solids, and dumping the liquid residue "well into the bay."

A dramatic improvement may have come temporarily in about 1921 when impediments (the shallows near 14th Avenue and the dam by Miami Lock No. 1) to free flow of fresh water from the Everglades were removed.

As of 1925, a comprehensive sewage disposal system was being planned that would take Miami's sewage to the Gulf Stream. By then, 60 unscreened sanitary sewers dumped into the bay and river and there was a separate storm sewer system. This pollution of the river had become a recognized health hazard and the odors were well noted. In 1934, an expensive city sewer project was considered, Miami being one of a few cities of its size without a modern system of treating its sewage before discharge into the bay or river. Unfortunately, the good plans of 1925 and 1934 never saw fruition; probably because of the disastrous 1926 hurricane, followed by the Great Depression and World War II. By the 1950s, 41 sanitary sewers emptied into the bay and 29 into the river. It was a low point in Miami's history!

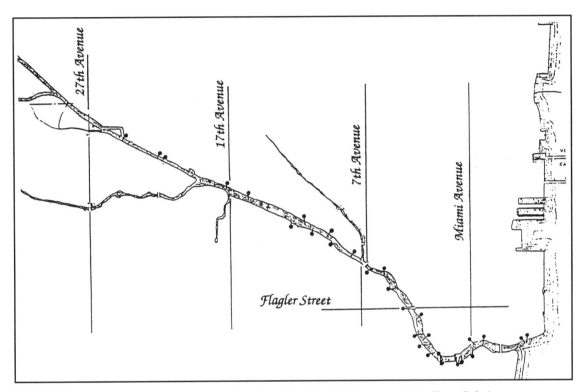

Figure 3B. Twenty-nine raw sewage outlets into the Miami River, ca. 1950. (Don Gaby)

A turnaround came during the 1950s when the county built a modern sewage treatment plant on Virginia Key and began to route all of the sanitary sewers to that plant from where the treated effluent was pumped out into the Gulf Stream. That restructuring of the system, a tremendous project, was accomplished over many years. Although some raw sewage occasionally reaches the river today, especially during heavy rain situations, that source of pollution has been largely eliminated. With respect to this type of pollution, the Miami River today is immensely cleaner than it was before.

For all of the above, many Miamians still remember swimming in the river with fondness. The author's memory of the river began in the late 1930s and 1940s, when as a boy, he frequently watched the river below Miami Avenue. Certainly there near its mouth the river was not fit to swim in. However, several prominent Miamians, who have or had businesses on the river, tell about how as boys during that same period they often dove off or near the sanitary sewer outlets and simply pushed the excrement and other waste out of the way. None was ever known to become ill from that practice.

Figure 3C. Metropolitan Dade County's modern sewage treatment plant on Virginia Key, ca. 1963. (Romer Collection, Miami-Dade Public Library)

Upstream conditions were undoubtedly better, improving as one went up the river. Two river businessmen described the river as yellowish in color up to about 17th Avenue, then markedly cleaner. The south fork was cleaner for much longer and there was a favored swimming spot below the 22nd Avenue bridge. On the north fork, the last of the city's sanitary sewer outlets was near 22nd Avenue, just below where the Miami Canal joins the river. In about 1921, the gates of Miami Lock No. 1 and the associated dam on the Miami Canal near 33rd Avenue were removed. About the same time, the shallow area in the river near 14th to 15th Avenues was also removed to improve drainage from the Everglades. During the 1920s and into the 1940s, flow from the Everglades was uncontrolled. That unrestricted flow probably helped reduce the pollution except during periods of drought. It might explain how, in the early 1920s, the Miami Canoe Club was formed with a clubhouse on the river below Flagler Street. Nicely dressed people were photographed in their canoes on that part of the river, evidently with little fear of spilling into the water. In swimming attire, some members of the club practiced "hurdling" their canoes, running one canoe upon another, surely with frequent spills into the river by their clubhouse. That apparent reduction in pollution did not last as the city and pollution grew together rapidly. A salinity dam installed on the Miami Canal near 35th Street in 1945 again restricted the flow of fresh water and accelerated the increase in pollution for another decade or so.

Salt water intrusion is another form of pollution on the Miami River. When Everglades drainage began in 1906 during the administration of Governor Broward, some engineers realized that the drainage canals cut below sea level would invite salt water intrusion, if not dammed. Even dammed, drainage by the canals lowered ground-water levels in adjacent areas, disturbed the natural balance between the fresh ground water and the salt water of Biscayne Bay, and permitted salt water to locally intrude the permeable limestone.

By 1920, the city's fresh water well fields near today's Jackson Memorial Hospital were turning salty from heavy pumping even with the dam near 33rd Avenue. New wells were dug in Hialeah. Evidently the demand for rapid drainage in a flood took precedence over the long term danger of salt water intrusion, because the dam was removed around 1921. By 1945, salt water had intruded several miles up the Miami and Tamiami Canals. Some of the new wells in Hialeah had to be shut down. In 1945, a salinity control dam was installed on the Miami Canal near 35th Street, and others later were installed on the Tamiami Canal and at the end of the south fork of the river. These temporarily stopped the salt water intrusion, but flooding from two hurricanes in 1947 was not controlled well. (This disaster resulted in the formation of the Central and Southern Florida Flood Control District, today the South Florida Water Management District.)

With rapidly increasing population and demand for fresh water, something obviously had to be done. As early as 1946, money was appropriated for a new dam and boat lock just west of 27th Avenue. By the 1960s, a model for a Salinity Control Dam and Navigation Locks was prepared by the Metropolitan Dade County Public Works Department. An alternative solution to the problem was found by drilling new wells far to the southwest. But with Miami's population continuing to grow and demands for fresh water increasing with it, future historians may well record some drastic measure taken to alleviate this decades old problem.

Deepening and widening of the Miami River and Canal below 35th Street by the Corps of Engineers in the early 1930s left the main stream of the river essentially clear of sediment. Since that time, storm sewer runoff from city streets plus some sediment brought down the canals has heavily loaded the river system. Such sediment includes rubber and synthetic material from tires, carbon from aircraft and land vehicle exhausts, chemicals from the Everglades agricultural areas, old paint from boats, plus dirt, trash and debris of various sorts. Perhaps one fourth of the volume of the main stream of the river is occupied by such material. For a long time cleaning chemicals and oils from Miami International Airport drained into the river. Such pollutants from the Metro-Dade County bus maintenance facility on 32nd Avenue also drained directly into the river. As this is written, removal of the sediment is proposed, but again some future historian will have to record what is done.

We should note that the contribution from the storm sewer system is gradually being eliminated as old storm sewers are retrofitted with catchment basins designed to retain the first inch of runoff which is known to contain the vast majority of the contaminants. New construction includes this provision.

Probably from the beginning, some people carelessly or maliciously disposed of trash or unwanted items into the river. It is a matter of pride and community attitude. In the 1960s, a movement began for restoration of the Miami River. As part of that movement, a river businesswoman known as Kate Thornhill managed to have the county provide for a clean-up boat to clear debris from the surface of the river (see Chapter 20). A similar vessel operated until recently to keep the river's waters free of floating material. In the 1980s, an added attraction was headless chickens or other animals killed in the course of Santeria religious rites. Many people, even boaters, still dispose of unwanted items in the river as they do in the bay.

Historically, oil spills on the river have been a problem almost from the city's founding, certainly since the start of the Miami Canal. As early as the 1910s, there were occasional newspaper reports of oil spills on the river. These frequently resulted from leaky fuel barges or careless operators. Police protection was demanded, and in 1919 the Bowers-Southern Dredging Co. was charged with allowing fuel to leak, but the case was lost when no city ordinance could be cited. A particularly bad spill in 1922 covered the river with heavy crude oil from the fork (19th Avenue) all the way to the bay, causing considerable damage to boats. Boat owners complained that the stuff had to be scraped off, with their boats put in dry dock for cleaning. That deluge was said to be the third in as many weeks. As today, most spills, accidental or deliberate, probably went unreported.

By the late 1970s, when the author moved on the river, the major offenders were ocean freighters towed up the river to the shipping terminals on the Miami Canal, the so-called Port of the Miami River. These vessels sometimes pumped their bilges while in port, usually at night with an outgoing tide, causing one to believe that it was deliberate. In one such incident in 1980—when the Coast Guard was less occupied intercepting illegal drugs and aliens—federal agents traced an oil sample from the "spill" to the *M/V Hyber Trader*, with a fine assessed and collected from the vessel. (During 1982 the Coast Guard responded to 41 reported oil spills on the river.) As this is written a decade later, that problem continues and some sort of "river authority" is proposed with jurisdiction over all parts of the river system. Again, some future historian must record the solution to that problem.

Chapter 4
Claughton Island and Miami Center/Bayfront Park

Approaching the mouth of the Miami River from the south one sees Claughton Island just off-shore on the south side and Miami Center, adjacent to Bayfront Park, on the north side. Both are entirely artificial. The island is the older in its beginning.

When the Miami Canal opened in 1912 and the downstream portion of the river silted so heavily that it had to be dredged out, much of that sediment was placed to form two small spoil islands at the north end of today's Claughton Island. The origin of the larger island was undoubt-edly from dredging the river. The smaller island, somewhat farther offshore but closer to the main navigation channel, was said by one account to have come from digging out a vessel that went aground on that spot.

In 1871, Mary Brickell settled with her family on what soon became known as Brickell Point, where she helped build a home in the wilderness (see next chapter). By 1912, she was a very wealthy widow and lived in a beautiful mansion commanding a view of Biscayne Bay. She enjoyed an unobstructed view of the bay for over four decades until the Miami Canal opened and the two spoil islands formed. In the summer of 1914, Mrs. Brickell offered to remove the islands by the mouth of the river at her own expense. She wished to fill some low land by pumping the spoil onto it, and perhaps to restore her view of the bay. Many thought removal of the islands would improve navigation into and out of the river. However, some opposed her proposal. By 1916, the city came to her support as others pointed out that the islands were unsightly, a menace to navigation, and that they caused unpleasant odors in the vicinity of the Royal Palm Hotel. Dr. James Jackson, president of the Board of Health, declared the islands to be a menace to health.

In 1916, the trustees of the Florida Internal Improvement Fund (IIF) advertised to sell "A certain partially submerged tract or island, together with a certain submerged portion thereto contiguous, lying in Biscayne Bay, exact description not given, containing approximately 5 acres." (This tract did not include the smaller island.) Four bids ranged from just $10.10 per acre to $3,000 for the whole tract. Mrs. Brickell bid $750 and Mrs. M. R. Burlingame bid $3,000 for the whole tract. On 21 June 1916, the IIF trustees accepted Mrs. Burlingame's bid and ordered a deed issued. She requested that the deed be issued to Ray G. and Margaret R. Burlingame.

Margaret Burlingame was a Miami businesswoman who came from Michigan, and was said to be the only woman owner of an advertising agency in the world. She helped Carl Fisher in promoting Miami Beach, but thought that winter visitors would always come and that Miami should be promoted for the year round resident. She wished to develop the two spoil islands into a much larger island where she might even build her home. By late June the deed had not been issued and Mrs. Brickell filed suit to enjoin the IIF trustees from deeding the two islands to Mrs. Burlingame. This began a long legal battle. The circuit court promptly ruled in support of the IIF trustees' right to sell. An appeal ended in 1918 when the Florida Supreme Court ordered the deed

Figure 4A. Aerial view of the Mrs. Burlingame Islands and the Royal Palm Hotel marina looking northwest, 1924. (Romer Collection, Metro-Dade Public Library)

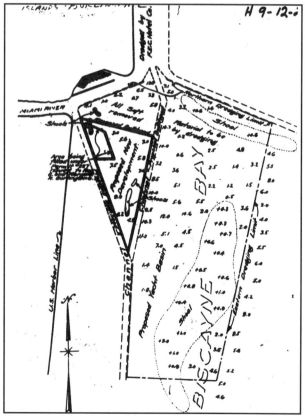

Figure 4B. *Miami Herald* map of proposed 5- and 21-acre islands, 1925. (Metro-Dade Public Library)

delivered to Mrs. Burlingame. On early maps these two small islands appear as the "Mrs. Burlingame Islands."

In 1920, Mrs. Burlingame declared her intention to build a magnificent hotel or apartment house. In 1921, a "5-1/4 Acre Island With Permit To Fill Facing the Royal Palm Hotel" was advertised. A permit from the War Department (today we would say Army Corps of Engineers) in April 1922 required bulkheading and filling of a five acre island to be completed by the end of 1922. Thus began Burlingame Island, as it would be known until well after World War II.

Mrs. Burlingame never built anything on the island that came to bear her name. Evidently she obtained an extension of time because a new permit #257 was issued in April 1923 and photographs show that nothing was done by 1924. The

Burlingames sold to E. J. Reed of Miami, president of the Beacon Realty Corp., who in 1925 applied for permission to fill a much larger, triangular-shaped island. Such permission must have been denied. By the end of 1925, bulkheading had begun for filling the island of five acres that was originally permitted. Interestingly, it was a trapezoid-shaped island that included the southern half of the larger spoil island, but the smaller one that was farther offshore was not included even though it was closer to the navigation channel in the river. Trees grew on the 5-acre island by 1928 and the two little spoil islands were gone.

Figure 4C. Initial 5-acre "Burlingame Island" under construction as seen over the Royal Palm Hotel, 1925, looking southeast. (Historical Museum of Southern Florida)

R. P. Clark, whose dredging company enlarged the island to 20.7 acres in 1932, owned it until A. Frank Katzentine and Julio Sanchez acquired it in January 1937. (Katzentine was an attorney, once mayor of Miami Beach, and Sanchez a Cuban sugar plantation operator. Both lived on Miami Beach.) In November 1943, Mrs. Edward N. Claughton and her son Jr. bought it. For almost half a century, from the 1920s into the 1970s, Burlingame Island—as it was still known—provided shelter for small boats coming to the river from the south. The author, like many others, used to drop his sail in the lee of the island before motoring up the river. The island also became a paradise for rats and raccoons who would eye passing boaters with suspicion.

Development of Burlingame Island continued to be controversial. The Florida Supreme Court in 1955 denied Claughton's claim to more land while affirming the 20.7 acres because back in 1932 the city had encouraged the owners to have it bulkheaded to accept spoil from the Corps of Engineers dredging the river. By 1965, permission was obtained to enlarge the island—then owned jointly by Claughton and J. A. Frates—to 44 acres between the existing three navigation channels. A causeway led to the island from the foot of S.W. 8th Street by 1975 and development began in earnest. Unfortunately, this low, fixed bridge blocked the passage of all but the smallest boats. A group of high-rise condominiums, two hotels, and over a million square feet of office space were planned, plus a 3.5 acre public park. Development continues today with a combination of luxury condominium apartment towers and townhouses plus an executive office complex known as the

Courvoiser Center—but no public park. It is a development of which Mrs. Burlingame would be proud. However, because the condominium has unfortunately taken the name "Brickell Key," some people mistake that for the name of the island. Surely it is an appellation that Mary Brickell herself never would have approved!

See Figure 4B for the original two small spoil islands and the proposed larger islands of about five and 21 acres. Figure 2D shows the completed larger "Burlingame Island." The map at the end of the book shows today's Claughton Island of 44 acres.

Miami Center and Bayfront Park

The story of Miami Center and Bayfront Park is not so controversial. Together they drastically altered the shoreline where the river once opened gently toward the northeast. Planning for a bayfront park began in the mid 1910s. By the end of that decade, the downtown bayfront had become a colorful but not beautiful collection of piers, houseboats, yachts, etc. The "et cetera" included Flagler's old Stone Dock with the Fair Building just below Flagler Street, Matthew Elser's entertainment pier on an extension of Flagler Street, Captain Tom Newman's pier with his charter fishing boats including the 84-foot *Kewah,* and the Biscayne Bay Yacht Club on a pier at N.E. 1st Street. (Captain Newman came to Miami in 1903 and took charters to places like Flagler's Long Key Fishing Camp. In 1923, he proposed a design for the new Bay Front Park—the early name had three words—that was quite close to the final professional design adopted.) The et cetera also included some 50 houseboats of all sizes and descriptions—some considered an eyesore, some too old to move, plus the stench of the sewer dumping into the bay at the shoreline.

By May 1920, the City of Miami had agreed to purchase the narrow strip of land between Bayshore Drive and Biscayne Bay, from Flagler Street north to 6th Street, with an option to buy the similar strip along the shore south to S.E. 2nd Street.

There was some trouble with Locke T. Highleyman about the purchase of Elser's Pier. At that time Highleyman owned a three-quarter interest in the Pier and served as trustee for Fred W. Maxwell who owned the remaining quarter interest. Highleyman opposed the new system of street numbering adopted by the City Council and endorsed by the postal authorities in 1920, and tried to renege on a contract he made with the City of Miami in 1921 to sell the Pier for $175,000. It may have been a family squabble, with his wife claiming that she had not signed the contract, but in addition, the contract was poorly drawn. In May 1924, negotiations failing, the city filed a condemnation suit in order to save time. Bulkheading had already begun! In July, Highleyman bought Maxwell's quarter interest for $100,000. In November, with filling underway, the condemnation jury set a value of $379,000 on the pier property, and the city moved promptly to acquire it at that price. Highleyman still claimed it was worth far more than that, and threatened an appeal to a higher court. But he slept on that notion and the next day announced that he would give up the fight.

A bond issue in 1921 allowed purchase of the strip north of Flagler Street from the Florida East Coast Railway Company in 1922 for $1,000,000. The piece south to S.E. 2nd Street was obtained in 1924. In this way, the city acquired about half a mile of bayshore and decided to fill about 1,000 feet out from shore to the recently established harbor line.

What of the area south of the planned Bayfront Park?

This property was owned by the Florida East Coast Hotel Company, founded by Henry Flagler. *The Metropolis* reported in February 1922 that the *Waldeck-Deal* dredge began filling the old "swash channel" along the bayfront at the Royal Palm. That was the start of this grand bayfront development!

In Chapter 2 we noted that when the Royal Palm Hotel was built in 1896, its marina consisted of a single long pier at a slight angle to the curving shoreline. By 1907, Flagler built a larger marina consisting of three piers at an acute angle to the shoreline running out from an area of fill that extended some 95 feet into the river. The land being filled east of the Royal Palm Hotel grounds and south of S.E. 2nd Street in 1922 would include a much larger marina of 10 piers extending out toward the southeast and protected by a long pier that ran east-northeast from the old marina fill and along the harbor line in the river. Construction of the new marina included entirely filling what had been the marina of 1907. Aerial photographs show that by March 1924, the dredge had filled a large area east from the Royal Palm Hotel grounds and connected it to the mainland with a road. By year's end it was complete, extending east about 1,000 feet to the harbor line in the bay.

This large parcel remained largely undeveloped except for the Royal Palm Hotel marina and a new Biscayne Bay Yacht Club (BBYC) building facing east at the edge of the bay. Forced to abandon their clubhouse on a pier near the foot of N.E. 1st Street, the BBYC engaged architects Hampton and Ehman to design a new clubhouse on the new land being filled only three blocks south. In the popular Spanish style, this three-story building was constructed of reinforced concrete and hollow tile with a barrel tile roof. (See Figure 2E and others.) It took the brunt of the 1926 hurricane with no exterior damage—a tribute to its solid construction. This beautiful new clubhouse served its members only five years. With the BBYC behind in paying its landlord and the sheriff preparing to padlock their clubhouse, the BBYC moved out under cover of darkness on New Year's Eve, 1930. Several prominent members used Hugh Matheson's motorized barge to transport the club's belongings upriver (see Chapter 8). During the 1930s, their former clubhouse on the bayfront became a popular nightclub and gambling casino, known as the Royal Palm Club. (By then the Royal Palm Hotel itself was gone.) Both the marina and the nightclub were taken over by the Coast Guard during World War II.

Following the war, many knew this land as "Ball Point" after Edward Ball, famous trustee for the Dupont estate which came to control both the Florida East Coast Railway and the Florida East Coast Hotel Co. He filled the marina, but the land remained undeveloped until the 1970s when Theodore Gould, a northern investor, built the large travertine-covered buildings that we see today. If you take the "Riverwalk" just south of the Intercontinental Hotel today, you pass along the line of the long pier of the former marina.

This area south of the line of S.E. 2nd Street was almost completely bulkheaded and filled before the development of Bayfront Park began. Several private citizens contributed ideas for the design of the new park. E. G. Sewell, chairman of the Chamber of Commerce, pushed for recreational facilities in the park. Capt. Tom Newman urged a proper yacht basin plus other amenities. The Women's Club wanted a large library and memorial to Henry Flagler. In June 1923, the houseboats and yachts were ordered to vacate. (Capt. Newman sold the *Kewah* and went into the ice making business; see Chapter 9.)

Figure 4D. Aerial of Florida East Coast Hotel Co. property and Bayfront Park, looking west, ca. 1925. (Florida State Archives)

The city wisely chose to hire a professional landscape architect, Warren H. Manning of Cambridge, Massachusetts, to provide the needed design. He provided a basic plan by early 1924. Manning's design incorporated some of the ideas previously presented by Miamians. It was a very good plan. The Comer-Ebsary Foundation Co. of Miami (see Chapter 16) began bulkheading in May 1924. Another Miami company, the Clark Dredging Co. (see Chapter 8), did the filling, completed in early 1925. Elser's Pier and the old Stone Dock and Fair Building were simply filled around. Not until September 1925 were they finally torn down as the park was landscaped. The park itself opened to the public the following year, just in time for the great hurricane of September 1926. That hurricane brought a storm surge of 11 feet to the mouth of the river, covering the park and the adjacent F.E.C. Hotel Co. property with numerous displaced ships and private yachts.

Miami's original Bayfront Park, although contributing to the drastic alteration of the shoreline where the mouth of the Miami River once opened gently to the northeast, was a great asset for the community. It provided much natural beauty with curving walks among a large variety of semi-tropical trees and palms. A bandshell at the south end was situated to allow visitors to enjoy the prevailing bay breeze. A yacht basin could accommodate 130 boats. In time, more plants were added, plus a lovely sunken garden, and many markers, statues, and monuments pertinent to Miami's history. There was a clear view down Flagler Street to the bay and beyond. After World War II, a library was built in the park that blocked the view from Flagler Street. That view was restored when the building was demolished and the library moved to the new Cultural Center on West Flagler Street in the early 1980s. But today the view is again blocked by large buildings of the Dodge Island seaport. More recent "improvements" have included removing many of the statues and monuments together with much of the natural beauty.

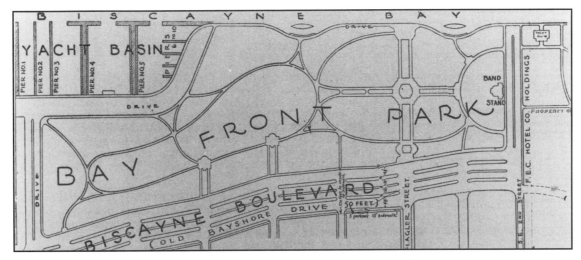

Figure 4E. Design of Bayfront Park, from City Managers Report, 1926. North is to the left. (Historical Museum of Southern Florida)

Figure 4F. Sunken Garden in Bayfront Park, ca. 1950. (Historical Museum of Southern Florida)

Chapter 5
Mouth of the Miami River to Brickell Avenue
(S.E. 2ⁿᵈ Avenue)

Juan Ponce de Leon discovered Florida and Biscayne Bay in 1513 and probably visited the Tequesta Indian village at the mouth of the Miami River on its north shore. The Tequesta were the native Indians of southeast Florida with many villages in the area, and were related to the Calusa tribe of the west coast. Just as the Miami was the principal stream along the southeast coast, their village at the mouth of the river was their largest.

The Tequesta were a primitive people with crude structures of wood and thatch who never developed agriculture and lived primarily from gathering fruits, hunting and fishing. They built large canoes that allowed them to sail well offshore. Over the many centuries of their occupation, they built a very large midden or burial mound, some 100 feet long and standing 20-25 feet above sea level. That midden was located right at the shore of Biscayne Bay, where today the Southeast Financial Center building is again the highest man-made structure around.

(Much of the prehistoric and pre-1896 history of the area around the mouth of the Miami River was concentrated downstream from today's Miami Avenue. The line of today's S.E. 2nd Avenue is an unrealistic artificial divider and will be ignored only in this chapter for this earlier period. The reader should bear this in mind while reading the early portions of Chapters 5 and 6 relating to this area.)

The Tequesta Indian village of the 16th century was located on the north shore of the river and extended from Biscayne Bay westward to near today's Miami Avenue.

During the first 250 years of Spanish possession, the Spanish attempted unsuccessfully to establish a mission here on the Miami River. In 1567, a Jesuit, Brother Francisco Villareal, established the first mission near today's Hyatt Regency Hotel. The Indians helped him to erect a large cross and to build 28 simple houses within a stockade. However, discontent among the military garrison stationed there due to the mosquitoes, sandflies, horseflies, boredom and the long, hot summer led the soldiers to harass the Indians and brought abandonment of this effort. Reestablished the following year, the mission lasted only into 1570. The Tequesta seemed not to make good converts to Christianity. Sadly, their numbers were greatly reduced by the introduction of European diseases such as smallpox.

In 1743, the Spanish tried again. Fathers Joseph Maria Monaco and Joseph Xavier de Alana, together with more soldiers, built another mission. This time it was more substantial, a triangular fort which they christened "Pueblo de Santa Maria de Loreto." It was the first European name for what we now call Miami. However, that mission was also ill-fated. With the Indians now hostile rather than friendly, the new settlement was abandoned after just six months. Florida became a British possession in 1763. Fearing the British who might take them for slaves, many Tequestas asked to be taken to Cuba with the departing Spaniards. (In 1711, some Tequestas emigrated to

Cuba under pressure from invading Creeks from the north who, having learned from British colonists the status attached to owning slaves, often enslaved the Tequesta they captured.) In contrast to modern times, these early migrations of refugees were from (today's) Miami to Havana. For a brief period toward the end of the 18th and start of the 19th century there were few, if any, Indians in the region of the Miami River.

After the Spanish left in 1763, the British surveyed Biscayne Bay but no settlements were established on the bay or on the Miami River. During the second Spanish period, 1784-1821, non-Spanish people were encouraged to settle here and some came from the Bahamas. John Egan received a grant of 100 acres on the north bank of the river near its mouth. After Florida became a United States Territory in 1821, his son James Egan (a/k/a Hagan) received a grant of 640 acres on the north bank of the river that included his father's 100 acres. His widowed mother, Rebecca Egan, received 640 acres on the south bank. The chain of title to much downtown Miami property begins with the Egans (or Hagans).

The most prominent of the early settlers was Richard Fitzpatrick. In 1830, he came to the Miami River from Columbia, South Carolina, via Key West where he was a prominent citizen. Originally a planter, Fitzpatrick bought the land on both sides of the Miami River near the bay and came with about 60 black slaves to develop a plantation. James Wright was his overseer. Many citrus trees and coconut palms were already bearing; and he cleared much additional land to grow sugarcane, corn, sweet potatoes, pumpkins, plantains and bananas. For livestock he had hogs, ducks, chickens, turkeys and guinea fowls. Fitzpatrick had a large frame plantation house on the north side of the river and kept most of his slaves on the south side—no doubt for security. There were 12 slave houses, plus five other houses and a log cabin. It was a fine plantation in the wilderness.

After the Second Seminole War began in December 1835 and the Indians moved south, Fitzpatrick fled with his slaves and other possessions to the safety of Key West. Other settlers on the river followed his example, and with good reason! (The hurricane of September 1835, thought to have formed Norris Cut, probably flooded much of Fitzpatrick's plantation and may have given him a prior incentive to abandon his property on the river.) Fitzpatrick served during the war as aide-de-camp to both Generals Clinch and Call. After the war he moved to Texas.

The Seminole Wars (1835-1858) came about because of pressure from white settlers to take the traditional lands of the Seminoles (in Florida) and to reclaim runaway black slaves. The word "Seminole" comes from the Spanish word "cimarron" which meant runaway. It was applied both to Indians of the Creek nation who were forced into Spanish Florida by the British colonists of Georgia and South Carolina, and to runaway black slaves from those same and other southern states. (In Jamaica today, the word "maroone," a derivation of "cimarron," refers to the descendants of former runaway slaves.) The author uses the word "Seminole" in its broader sense of including both the Indians and their Negro allies. A major purpose of those wars was to reclaim or claim black slaves. It is noteworthy that two U.S. Secretaries of War during those conflicts, Joel R. Poinsett during the Second and Jefferson Davis during the Third, were both southern slaveholders themselves.

The aim of the U.S. Government was to kill or forcibly relocate the Seminoles to west of the Mississippi River (excepting black slaves returned to their owners). The Second Seminole War began with the famous massacre of Major Dade's military contingent in central Florida in December 1835. That action was followed in January 1836 with the massacre of the Cooley family on the New River in today's Fort Lauderdale, and later the burning of the Cape Florida lighthouse on Key Biscayne. The Seminoles also burned the Fitzpatrick plantation and all other properties on the Miami River.

In late 1837, Fort Dallas was established on the north shore of the Miami River near the old Indian midden. An Army post, it was named after a Navy officer, Commodore Alexander J. Dallas, in command of the Navy in Florida waters. Consisting of just three log houses, it was alternately occupied and abandoned for the next five years. A number of military expeditions into the Everglades or along the adjacent coasts departed from Fort Dallas. These were by both Army soldiers and Navy "swamp sailors," sailors newly trained to fight on the rivers or in the swamps of the Everglades. The Navy cut much wood along the banks of the Miami for use as fuel on their gunbarges.

Toward the end of the war, marines joined the soldiers and sailors stationed at Fort Dallas. Probably the most famous of their expeditions was that by Colonel William S. Harney, who in December 1840 led 90 men in 16 canoes from Fort Dallas up the Miami River and halfway across Florida to capture and kill Chekaika at his camp deep in the Everglades. (Chekaika was chief of the "Spanish Indians," an isolated band thought by some to be a remnant of the old Calusa tribe.) Harney continued across the Everglades to enter the Gulf of Mexico via the river that ever since has carried his name. Harney and other officers demonstrated that the Army could follow the Seminoles anywhere in that vast expanse of wilderness. Many soldiers who later became famous—such as Joseph Johnson, Robert Anderson and Abner Doubleday—served at Fort Dallas.

For all the fighting elsewhere, there were only a few known fatalities resulting from military combat on the Miami River. One such fatality is well documented and is described in Chapter 14. In it Captain Samuel L. Russell was killed and later buried in the old Tequesta Indian midden at Fort Dallas (probably because the digging was easier there). Many other soldiers who died of illness also were buried in the midden. Knowledge of the other fatalities comes from an article in *The Miami Herald* of 1914. According to that account, Lieutenant Cates and several soldiers were wounded in a skirmish at Wagner's Spring (near today's Wagner Creek). As was the custom, the wounded soldiers were lying to rest below a large rubber tree (*Ficus aureum*) on the post near the old Indian midden where they could enjoy the cooling bay breeze. While thus resting, they were attacked and killed by Indians. (This was probably 1st Lt. Thomas Casey, posted at Fort Dallas in March 1839 but sent to Picolata because of illness. He was not wounded fatally, although others may have been. Even today newspapers are known occasionally to misspell a name or confuse some detail.) The "old rubber tree" was a monument later on the grounds of the Royal Palm Hotel. It fell quite suddenly one day in April 1914.

The Second Seminole War ended in December 1842. Approximately 6,000 Indians and a handful of Negroes were killed or removed from Florida. Some 1,500 soldiers died in the effort, plus an equal number disabled by wounds or illness. One soldier died or was disabled for every two Seminoles killed or forcibly removed! It was a terrible price to pay in lives and property lost, families disrupted and money. In the end, the government decided that it was not worth the cost and simply withdrew. Several hundred Seminoles remained deep in the Everglades.

An incidental benefit of the Second Seminole War was that the first official weather observations in the area that would become Miami—made by the post surgeon—began in 1839.

In 1842, the Congress passed the Armed Occupation Act, designed to encourage settlement in areas of conflict by granting 160 acres of land to anyone willing to move into Indian territory at least two miles from a military post and work the land for five years. Many new settlers came to the river. Richard Fitzpatrick sold his plantation lands on the Miami River to his nephew, William F. English. English, also from South Carolina, arrived with about 100 slaves to develop his plantation. He also had other ideas.

On the south shore he laid out the Village of Miami with named streets and lots to sell. It was the first use of "Miami" for the area. English also built a "coontie" mill on Wagner Creek, more than a mile upriver. The production of starch from the tubers of the native coontie plant (*Zamia pumila*) that grew profusely in the pine woods was almost the only means by which the early settlers could earn cash. Digging the tubers from the rocky land was laborious; grinding, separating and washing them was equally laborious and required an abundance of fresh water.

Dr. Robert R. Fletcher, a physician by profession and a prominent citizen of Key West, moved with his wife and two daughters to the Miami River in 1843. Mrs. Fletcher was a Spanish woman and they had the first mango on their place, probably brought from Cuba. Fletcher also introduced the guava to this country. He bought 10 acres on the south shore just east of today's Miami Avenue and opened a store. Here he had some 400 hogs, hundreds of chickens and many turkeys. Upstream on the south fork he purchased 160 acres and installed a coontie mill. It may have been the second such mill on the river. In 1844, "Miami" became the county seat and the courthouse

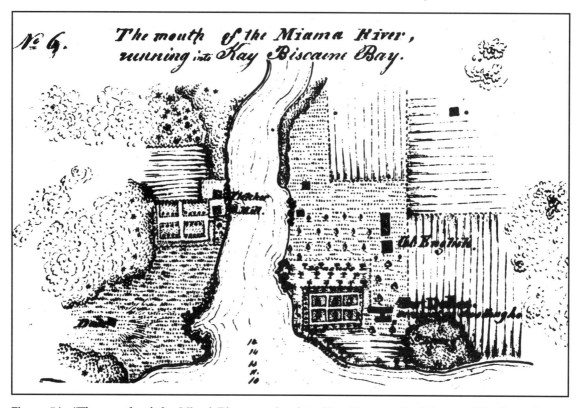

Figure 5A. "The mouth of the Miami River running into Key Biscayne Bay" from a U.S. Coast Survey map of February 1849. (Historical Museum of Southern Florida)

was in Fletcher's home. Fletcher sold his 10 acres to a family named Parsons in 1870, who in turn sold to a Mrs. Gilbert from New York who came with her daughter to spend the winters. The photograph in Figure lB was taken from her wharf. Other settlers were putting down roots in various places up the river during the mid 1840s. A survey made in early 1849 shows what was at the mouth of the river at that time.

In Figure 5A, make special note of the oval-shaped mound marked "limes" at the shore of Biscayne Bay which is the old Tequesta Indian midden, the town and some of the plantation, the two buildings of Fort Dallas from the Second Seminole War and two buildings of Col. English (whether he was a real colonel is a question). Construction of English's two buildings began in the late 1840s. The square building was a two-story stone structure intended for his plantation house and was later made much longer. The author calls it the "tall building." The longer building next to it, a one-story stone structure, was intended for slave quarters. Probably it was meant for house slaves, as English would have kept most of his slaves across the river for security as his uncle had done. The author calls this the "long building."

An Indian scare in 1849 combined with the discovery of gold in California caused many settlers to leave the river. English went west to seek his fortune in the California gold fields. While there, he accidentally shot himself to death getting off his horse. On the Miami River, the Army again occupied Fort Dallas in September 1849 with more than 100 soldiers. They completed the two stone buildings begun by English, and repaired the log houses left before. But the Army's stay was unproductive and they left at the end of 1850.

The Third Seminole War should never have happened. It began in December 1855 when Lt. Hartsuff, with a surveying party near the border of the Big Cypress and the Everglades, destroyed "for fun" a patch of bananas that had been carefully nurtured by Chief Holatter Micco (Billy Bowlegs). Thus provoked, Micco attacked the soldiers and war was declared again almost immediately. This time the war lasted only 29 months. Only a few Seminoles were killed or captured, but the soldiers extensively damaged Seminole crops and homes in the Everglades. That war ended in April 1858.

At Fort Dallas, the Third Seminole War offered an excellent example of Parkinson's sixth law at work. (To paraphrase, this law states that organizations often do their best work when understaffed, poorly equipped and with inadequate facilities; and that they often acquire sufficient people, equipment and facilities when the need for them is gone.) Whereas most of the bloody fighting was done during the long Second Seminole War, when Fort Dallas consisted of just three temporary buildings, during the Third Seminole War the Army reoccupied Fort Dallas again and enlarged it on a grand scale. The two stone buildings begun originally by William English for his plantation, and completed by the Army in 1849, were renovated and made larger. The "tall building" was used for troop quarters, and the "long building" for a warehouse with troops on a temporary second story. There were 20 buildings, including a hospital, four officers quarters facing the parade ground by the bayshore, magazine, guardhouse, office, three kitchens, a bake house, stable, blacksmith shop, carpentry shop, storehouse and a forage house. There was a broad parade ground along the bayshore with the flag flying proudly at the water's edge. At least three companies were posted there. The soldiers were kept moving about the area to impress the Seminoles, making several expeditions into the Everglades. Fort Dallas was never a true defensive

Figure 5B. Artist's drawing of old Fort Dallas, ca. 1869. (Florida State Archives)

fort, but more of a materials depot and staging area for troops. One benefit of this Third Seminole War was that the interior of peninsula Florida, unknown before these wars, was mapped for the first time.

Those few settlers left on the Miami River during the Civil War period (1861-1865) were isolated by the Union blockade, deprived of some essential needs and contact with the outside world. Some of the more adventurous occasionally ran the blockade to bring supplies from the Bahamas. That irked the Union commander. On one occasion, Capt. English of the blockade ship *Sagamore* sent a gunboat up the Miami River. They stopped at Dr. Fletcher's store to demand that he swear allegiance to the federal government—which, as a Confederate sympathizer (his son Robert was in the Confederate army), he refused to do. Farther upstream they burned the home of a suspected blockade runner, George Lewis, with the smoke clearly visible from the mouth of the river. Returning downriver, they again demanded that Dr. Fletcher swear allegiance—which, upon further consideration, he did. Lewis ended the war in federal prison.

The old Fort Dallas buildings were used by various people after the war. The property was occupied illegally by William Gleason, who in the late 1860s served as county clerk and county tax accessor. Dr. J. V. Harris purchased the property on the north bank in 1869, and forced Gleason off the land. There was yet another Indian "scare" in 1873. Two companies of soldiers returned to Fort Dallas the following year. All of the wooden buildings of Fort Dallas burned that year. Also in 1874, the Biscayne Bay Company purchased the Fort Dallas tract.

Julia Tuttle, later to be known as "the mother of Miami," bought the land on the north side of the river in 1887. In 1891, she moved into the old Fort Dallas "tall building," begun by English in the late 1840s for his plantation house. Tuttle improved the structure for her home, and made it the center of social activity on the north side until the founding of the city.

Figure 5C. Old Fort Dallas "tall building," ca. 1885. (Florida State Archives)

East of Today's S.E. 2nd Avenue

Modern Miami began as a dream of Julia Tuttle, a wealthy widow who in 1887 purchased about a square mile of land (640 acres) on the north shore of the Miami River near its mouth, including old Fort Dallas. In 1891 she moved to this area from Cleveland, where she had been an old friend of John D. Rockefeller. Tuttle helped induce Henry M. Flagler to bring his Florida East Coast Railway to the Miami River by giving him much land for a grand hotel at the mouth of the river plus half of the remainder of her property—not counting her own homesite. William Brickell (see below) contributed land on the south side of the river in addition to other land he gave Flagler in today's Fort Lauderdale. Henry Flagler provided both the capital and the capability to make it all happen. Tuttle's agreement with Flagler was specific on many points, including what was to be done and how soon. Among other things, Flagler was to bring his railroad to the Miami River, build a grand hotel and lay out the infant city. (Flagler was planning to extend his railroad to Key West as early as 1891. Great freezes in north and central Florida during the winter of 1894-95 also influenced his decision.)

Many have called Henry Flagler a "robber baron." If he was that, he must have been among the best of the breed. The author prefers to think of him differently. Henry Flagler was a partner with John D. Rockefeller and held the second most shares of the Standard Oil Company, making him one of the wealthiest men in the country. He began building his railroad and hotels down the east coast of Florida at an age when most wealthy men would have been happy to retire. He built them with his own money, and whatever he built was made to last. He treated his employees fairly and paid them well—a rarity in those days—and he was very generous with his friends and the Miami community. He made some mistakes—one might cite the narrow streets of the original City of Miami, and lack of parks—but he certainly did not lack vision. Taking his railroad on to Key West—creating what some described as an "eighth wonder of the world"—was proof enough of his vision and the courage and daring of a much younger man.

Flagler's men arrived to clear the land for the new city of Miami and to begin construction of his Royal Palm Hotel at the mouth of the river in March 1896, one month before the first train chugged into the settlement. His men cleared the land, laid out a city and built what was said to be one of the largest wooden buildings in the world in less than ten months! Situated about midway between the river and today's S.E. 2nd Street and just east of S.E. 2nd Avenue, the hotel was surrounded by spacious landscaped grounds extending to the river and bay and north to today's Flagler Street. (Unfortunately, in preparing the hotel site, they removed the old Tequesta midden. Human bones found in the midden, probably from both Indians and former soldiers, were placed in barrels and buried in a hole which has never been discovered.)

The Royal Palm Hotel was 680 feet long (more than twice the length of a footfall field), 267 feet wide and five stories tall overall, with a taller central tower and rotunda walk six stories above the ground. A broad veranda 800 feet long surrounded the entire eastern portion of the structure. There were 450 rooms, 100 with private bath, a grand ballroom, magnificent dining rooms and a huge lobby, all elegantly furnished. Elevators were provided. The hotel had its own electricity, ice and laundry plants. Located next to the hotel on the north side was a large casino with a swimming pool 140 feet long by 50 feet wide, 3-1/2 feet deep at one end to 6-1/2 feet deep at the other, filled with salt water from the bay and heated to 78° F. Painted Flagler's favorite color of yellow with green trim and a red mansard roof, the hotel rose in the wilderness to dominate the scene for the next three decades. It is difficult today to appreciate the spectacular way in which Miami got its start!

Figure 5D. The Royal Palm Hotel, ca. 1900. (Florida State Archives)

Guests of the Royal Palm Hotel included the wealthiest and most powerful people in the country. Many came in their own private railroad cars, arriving on a spur of the railroad that ran directly to the hotel. Others came in their private yachts, in that era representing some of the finest ships afloat. The hotel opened its doors for the first time on 16 January 1897 for a short season that lasted until March. By the summer of 1897, Miami's population had grown to some 2,000 people. The Royal Palm was Miami's premier hotel at least until the McAllister Hotel opened in late 1919, perhaps even after that. (The McAllister Hotel formerly stood on the site of today's "Columbus Bazaar," but was demolished in 1989.) The Royal Palm continued prominent until the great hurricane of September 1926. Downtown Miami was just within the "eye" wall and felt the full force of the storm. There was not so much wind damage, but the storm surge raised the level of the bay 11 feet at the mouth of the river, completely inundating the grounds. The hotel operated for two more seasons, closing after the winter of 1927-28. One should note that during all this time, there was no bridge crossing the river on S.E. 2nd or Brickell Avenue. Most people crossed on Miami Avenue.

As early as March 1925—at the peak of the 1920s building boom and before the famous hurricane—"south side" citizens petitioned for a bridge to cross the Miami River on Brickell Avenue to S.E. 2nd Avenue. It would carry a trolley line to connect with Coral Gables. Voting Miamians approved that bridge plus four others in a Harbor Bond Issue of February 1926. In 1928, the city appropriated money to purchase a strip of land along S.E. 2nd Avenue from the Florida East Coast Hotel Co. that owned the Royal Palm Hotel, plus payment to the company for removing the west end of the hotel that encroached on the street right-of-way. The F.E.C. Hotel Co. agreed to remove that portion of the hotel by August. How much was removed is not certain, but it appears to have been about 30 feet from the hotel and 10 feet from the swimming pool casino— only a small fraction of the structure and not evident in later aerial photographs. This alteration of the hotel revealed the two cylinder Westinghouse No. 18 gasoline engine used to power the generator that provided electricity for the Royal Palm Hotel and the City of Miami from 1899 until 1906. The carpenters engaged in the work remarked on the expert workmanship of those who built the hotel in 1896, and the excellent quality of the lumber after some 32 years. That good lumber went into many Miami homes.

In August 1928, the F.E.C. Hotel Co. decided to close the hotel for the coming winter season. Three factors played in that decision. First was the death of Joseph P. Reaves, hotel manager for more than 20 years who had a personal and loyal following in the face of decreased patronage. Second was that Miami's younger visitors preferred to patronize more modern hotels. And third was the removal of the building's west end. Never did the Royal Palm's established customers give way to modern innovations. Life went on serenely within its walls and gardens, and the same big opening parties marked the start of Miami's social season each year. It was the rendezvous for the rich and famous of a more genteel period. The Royal Palm was beloved by many older Miamians. Unfortunately, they were too few to sustain the hotel operation.

In September 1929, *The Miami Herald* announced that the "Old Royal Palm Hotel" would reopen for one night—to be Friday evening, 6 December 1929. A group of Miamians, with the concurrence of W. R. Kegan, Jr., president of the F.E.C. Hotel Co. and Flagler heir, planned this event. It was to be the Royal Palm's last bow to the "new Miami," and the entertainment planned around that theme would benefit the Children's Home Society. The date was chosen in conjunction with the University of Florida vs. University of Oregon football game scheduled the following day. For that event, they built a small stadium on N.W. 7th Street. *The Herald* never reported the gala evening, perhaps because the excessive cost of refurbishing the two-year vacant hotel for only a few hours of use prevented the event from ever taking place. However, the football game was played in the new stadium with Florida defeating Oregon 20 to 6. The enthusiastic crowd plus inadequate seating for that game inspired the move for a better stadium that culminated in today's famous Orange Bowl.

In March 1930, the city issued a permit for demolition of the Royal Palm Hotel. The demolition began that month and took most of the summer. For more than a decade afterward, the "footprint" of that grand old hotel could easily be seen in aerial photographs.

Initially, the Royal Palm Hotel's marina consisted of a single long pier extending into the river at a small angle to the curving coastline and a boathouse by the river's edge. Large yachts anchored in the bay. The hurricane of October 1906, which devastated the "Overseas Extension" of Flagler's railroad under construction in the Keys, passed directly over Miami—the calm of the eye lasting 30 minutes—severely damaging that first marina. By January 1907, Flagler interests built a larger marina consisting of three short piers, also at a slight angle to the shoreline, but extending out from an area of fill with a boathouse at the river's edge. As noted previously, this filling for the second marina reduced the width of the mouth of the river by some 95 feet. In 1924, with Miami enjoying the boom of the "Roaring '20s" and the demise of the hotel near but yet unsuspected, the Florida East Coast Hotel Co. built an even larger marina as described in Chapter 4.

Figure 5E. Original Royal Palm Hotel marina, ca. 1902. (Historical Association of Southern Florida)

Note in Figure 5F the original shoreline of the mouth of the river around the green grounds of the Royal Palm Hotel, marking an almost perfect quarter-circle. That original shoreline may also be seen in Figure 2C of Chapter 2 from 1940 with the hotel long gone but its "footprint" still evident. Everything seaward of that line was constructed later.

Figure 5F. The Royal Palm Hotel and marina, 1924. (Romer Collection, Metro-Dade Public Library)

Today's Dupont Plaza Hotel went up after World War II. It sits on what formerly were the riverfront grounds of the Royal Palm Hotel. As this is written, plans are being discussed for a new structure to take its place.

On the South Side of the River

A Tequesta Indian village also stood on the south shore near the river's mouth. Archaeological evidence indicates that it lasted from about 750 B.C. to about 1,200 A.D., after which the Indians lived only on the north shore.

William B. Brickell first came to the Miami River from Cleveland, Ohio, with Ephrain T. Sturtevant in 1870. (Sturtevant was the father of Julia Tuttle; he settled up the bay at Biscayne.) He purchased all of William English's land south of the river, except Dr. Fletcher's 10 acres, then returned in 1871 with his wife, Mary, two daughters, housekeeper and governess for the girls. Brickell was a world traveler who went to California for the gold rush and on to Australia where he met and married Mary Bulmer in 1855. Their arrival on the Miami River brought them to a whole new way of life. Together they built a home in the wilderness and began a trading business with the Indians and the few settlers then in the area.

Their trading post or store was the third on the Miami River, but very well situated and the only one to last into the 20th century. It was in their two-story house, set well back from the river

Figure 5G. Brickell's warehouse building and wharf, ca. 1908. (Thelma Peters, from a double postcard)

and bayshore, so Mary could attend to business when her husband was away. In 1873, it included the post office, served by the mail boat which came about once a week. In 1889, near the point where the south shore of the river reaches the bay which ever since has carried his name—Brickell built a building of two stories that was a warehouse on the ground floor with rooms to rent to winter visitors on the second floor. Open porches faced the bay on both floors. Even today, the configuration of the river's shoreline near Brickell Point is little changed (although the bayshore south of Brickell Point has been straightened and filled to the harbor line).

Some Miamians still living remember the Brickells as very reserved and difficult to get to know. Several early anecdotes may reveal some of their character. Ralph Monroe, who came to the Miami River from Staten Island in 1877 and later settled in Coconut Grove, recalled rescuing Brickell's small sloop (as written in *The Commodore's Story*) in 1874 when it was stranded in New York's upper harbor during a gale with freezing temperature. Brickell showed Monroe a map of his property in Florida and offered him a piece of land as his thanks for saving his boat and cargo. When Monroe later arrived by steamer at Key West and booked passage on Brickell's schooner to the Miami River, he had to pay for the passage and never received the land previously offered. George Parsons, an educated man who lived on the river near Brickell Point in the mid-1870s, described Mrs. Brickell as "a vile woman" and Mr. Brickell "as not really a man and who should be wearing woman's clothing (from how he behaved)" and "mean and petty." Others complained of daughter Alice Brickell's performance as postmistress, because she gave people their mail—or didn't give them their mail— depending upon how she felt that day!

For all the trouble that some white people appear to have had with the Brickells, they enjoyed very friendly relations with the Indians who came to trade or visit at their store. There was a mutual respect and trust, and the Indians often referred to Mr. Brickell as their "White Chief." The Indians had always been friendly before white men took their lands, and they became friendly again after the Seminole Wars ended. The Indians poled their dugout canoes down the river from the Everglades, bringing pelts of deer, otter and raccoon, alligator hides, and egret plumes to sell. In return, they bought tools, ammunition, cloth, beads and hand-powered sewing machines. Rather than barter, they preferred to deal in silver or gold coin. As many as 20 dugouts in a day were reported at Brickell's dock. C. E. Thompson wrote that sometimes the Indians beached their dugouts near today's S.W. 2nd Avenue and walked down the south shore to Brickell's store.

Capt. William Brickell was a superb sailor. He bought his schooner *Ada* from the New York Yacht Club, she being a fast, prize-winning boat—one of the fastest boats of its class on the east coast. Soon after arriving on the river he sailed from Key West to Miami in "sun to sun;" that is, in 24 hours, a record unbroken for at least three decades. He regularly sailed to New York to purchase stock for his store.

In 1895, Brickell gave much land, together with Julia Tuttle, as an inducement for Henry Flagler to bring his railroad south. This included about 300 acres on the New River in today's downtown Fort Lauderdale, plus the right-of-way for Flagler's railroad south of the Miami River. At that time Brickell operated a ferry service across the Miami River, and understood that Flagler would build a bridge to span the river. Just what formal agreement they made is not known, but the bridge originally built at Avenue G (today's S.W. 2nd Avenue) was not satisfactory. It was a crude wooden draw-bridge, half a mile upstream, and would become unsafe within just a few years. This misunderstanding or deception left Brickell bitter and more withdrawn, although he was always difficult to know or get along with. Some say also that Flagler made Brickell angry by piling spoil dredged from the river onto Brickell's land. The author finds that difficult to accept,

Figure 5H. The Brickell mansion, ca. 1908. (Florida State Archives)

considering Brickell's strong character and 25 years of experience fending for himself in a wilderness and on the sea for all his needs. In any case, Brickell used that spoil to improve the road to Coconut Grove, today's Brickell Avenue.

By the turn of the century the Brickells were quite wealthy. On the river were two wharves and their warehouse building. In about 1906 they built a beautiful mansion facing the bay (about where the Sheraton Brickell Point Hotel is located today). It had a 15-foot hall running back from the east entrance, with a parlor and library on the left side and a living room and dining room on the right, plus a butler's pantry and servants' dining room. The kitchen and laundry were in a separate fireproof building with a "blow-way" porch between. Ten bedrooms occupied the upper floors. Eighty-three years old, William Brickell died in January 1908 after 37 years of residence there. He left his wife and seven children, six still living on the property. They demolished the old warehouse building in May 1909. In June 1910, the original house and store was removed to make room for a new residence. Then the Brickells built a third residence on the point. The following year, palms and shrubbery beautified Brickell Avenue—said to be the city's most beautiful street.

Mary Brickell was a shrewd businesswoman. In 1896, she sold south side business lots for a good price. She promoted many business ventures in Miami, including an early cigar factory. In 1912, she made a hard deal with James Deering, selling him 130 acres of land at $1,000 per acre in cash (almost $3,000,000 in today's money) before he could construct his famous Villa Vizcaya. (It was said that she did not care for the smooth ways of Paul Chalfin who represented Deering in that transaction; also that Deering had the cash aboard his yacht.) The story of her unfortunate encounter with Margaret Burlingame was told in Chapter 4. In the early 1920s, she personally managed the real estate development of the Brickell Hammock subdivision. Although she died in January 1922 before that grand project was completed, at least she did not live to see the start of Burlingame Island. Their daughter Alice, the pioneer postmistress, was accidentally electrocuted in September 1924. While walking from the mansion to the "new" residence, she stepped into an electric power line blown down in a wind storm. Carrying 2,200 volts, it killed her instantly. Their daughter Maude lived in the old mansion until it was demolished in the 1960s.

(The estate of Mary Brickell, finally settled in 1925, was reported to be worth $12,000,000 with six heirs to share. That was approximately equivalent to $230,000,000 in today's money!)

Brickell Point, with only three houses, remained largely wooded until after World War II. In 1950, the Brickell Point Apartments, six small three-story buildings with a swimming pool and a dock, were built on the river shore by the point. They occupied the space taken by the latest of the three Brickell houses. The Elk's Club then occupied the second house. The Brickell mansion came down in 1964. In the early 1990s, the City of Miami lost a golden opportunity to acquire this property for a park. (The Brickells gave land for a small city park on Brickell Avenue between S.E. 5th and 6th Streets; it also included a Brickell mausoleum. Owners of the Brickell Point property, which was much better located for a park but difficult to develop for commercial purposes, offered to trade that prime property for the little city park which could be developed for commercial use. Perhaps some Brickell cantankerousness was a factor in the failure of negotiations, because the terms of the deed to the little park required approval of the heirs for a swap. By then the mausoleum was vacant. Such a deal seemed very much in the public interest and harmful to no one.)

Figure 5I. Brickell Avenue bridge and Brickell Point, looking southeast, 1940. (Historical Association of Southern Florida.)

The Brickell Avenue or S.E. 2nd Avenue bridge is the first bridge on the Miami River from the bay, but it is a rather recent addition. It is one of four similar bridges built under the same Harbor Bond Issue of February 1926. Southside citizens petitioned for a bridge at that location in 1925. In 1928, the City of Miami bought a strip of land for this bridge from the Florida East Coast Hotel Co. (The winter season of 1927-28 was the Royal Palm Hotel's final operating season.) Harrington, Howard, and Ash, architects and consulting engineers of Kansas City, designed this bridge, as well as two others. The E. F. Powers Co. of West Palm Beach built the foundation and approaches. The Nashville Construction Co. built the spans. The bridge had three concrete arches on the south side, and two similar arches on the north side, for an overall length of 410 feet. The clearance between fenders was 94 feet. This was the second among the four new bridges to be completed, opening for traffic in April 1929.

Electricity powered this four-lane bascule bridge for many years. The motor controls were from an early Miami trolley car. In 1986, the Florida Department of Transportation (FDOT) renovated the bridge and converted it from electric to hydraulic power; while retaining the electric power for a back-up system.

A new bridge with a "signature" design is funded by the FDOT for construction in 1993-95. It will be somewhat higher and provide for six lanes. However, the outside northbound lane may not be completed until the Dupont Plaza Hotel complex is demolished and replaced with a new structure. The new bridge will include architectural embellishments reflecting some of the early history of this area. These will include a statue of a Tequesta Indian, plus sculptures of Brickell, Tuttle, Flagler and Marjory Stoneman Douglas; facing east, north, south and west, respectively.

Although Douglas is not a true pioneer of the city, not arriving in Miami until 1915, her famous bestseller book, *The River of Grass*, was a pioneering effort and set the stage for a series of private and governmental efforts to save the Everglades. Miami's modern and early histories are intimately connected to the Everglades, as we have seen.

The Brickell Avenue or S.E. 2nd Avenue bridge is painted orange. Every bridge on the mainstream of the Miami River system is being painted a distinctive color after the "rainbow plan" adopted in 1985 by the Miami River Coordinating Committee (MRCC), a quasi-governmental body of concerned citizens working for a better Miami River and community. The rainbow plan is designed to improve the aesthetic appeal of the river and its environs. Bridges are painted as routine maintenance is performed.

Chapter 6
Brickell Avenue (S.E. 2ⁿᵈ Avenue) to Miami Avenue

The "tall building" of old Fort Dallas that became Julia Tuttle's home was illustrated in Chapter 5—which treated the history before there was a Miami—because by the 20th century most people seemed to forget that it also was a part of old Fort Dallas. It was located near the north portion of today's Hyatt Regency Hotel and Knight Center. The "long building" that would forever be associated with old Fort Dallas was close by to the west-northwest, about where today one enters the Occidental Parc Suite Hotel on S.E. 4th Street. Both buildings were rotated slightly clockwise from north in order to face the river.

The Miami Holding Co., headed by T. W. Palmer, a "golfing star," purchased "Old Fort Dallas" in January 1925 for a hotel site. It was the last parcel of the original Julia Tuttle purchase to be sold. The "tall building"—Tuttle's former home begun for William English's plantation house and then a part of Fort Dallas—gave way for construction of the Patricia Hotel. In its final years it was the Flagler Memorial Library of the Miami Woman's Club, but so extensively improved as to appear quite modern.

The "long building," also much altered, became the Fort Dallas Tea Room in 1923. An entrance portico supported by two columns added on the riverside was built about 1905 and then it

Figure 6A. Old Fort Dallas "long building," ca. 1880. (Florida State Archives)

was entirely enclosed by a long screened veranda when it became the tea room, or restaurant. Fortunately, the building's historic character was recognized, and many joined together to save it from destruction for commercial use. In March 1925, Dr. R. C. Hogue of Norfolk, Virginia bought the property. Mrs. Lon Worth Crow, president of the Woman's Club, persuaded Dr. Hogue to donate the building; but it had to be removed promptly to make room for a hotel, and at a cost estimated at $7,000 (equivalent to about $125,000 in today's money). The City Commission provided a site up the river in today's Lummus Park. Mrs. Edwin B. Webb of the Woman's Club, joined by Mrs. Frederick M. Hudson, regent of the Everglades Chapter of the Daughters of the American Revolution (DAR), led a fund raising drive. Those three ladies and their two organizations were most responsible for saving the "long building" of old Fort Dallas. Attempts to move the old building in sections failed when the mortar crumbled. By mid-July it was taken apart stone-by-stone and rebuilt in the park in more-or-less its original condition. The Robert Clay Hotel came to occupy that historic site the following year.

During the five years between her coming to live on the Miami River in 1891 and the arrival of Flagler's railroad in 1896, Julia Tuttle greatly improved her new home and grounds. She made the house more comfortable and planted more fruit trees on the 13 acres that surrounded the house and ran down to the river's edge. Isolated from the world except by boat, she surely longed for the company to which she was accustomed.

As part of Julia Tuttle's contract with Henry Flagler, he placed his Royal Palm Hotel well back from the river so her view of the bay would not be obstructed. Thanks to her, early Miamians also enjoyed this stretch of the north shore of the river east of today's S.E. 2nd Avenue that remained a scene of natural beauty for more than three decades. Until completion of the bridge in 1929, S.E. 2nd Avenue dead-ended well north of the river.

Julia Tuttle (and the Brickells) opposed the consumption of alcoholic beverages and made sure that all land deeds in her part of Miami included a clause prohibiting the sale of liquor. To relieve a dry throat, early Miamians had to journey beyond the city limits, then about a mile. She lived only two years after the realization of her dream of founding a city by the Miami River. During that brief period she built a large frame hotel—the Miami Hotel—on Avenue D (Miami's first street that today is Miami Avenue), and bought more land in the surrounding country, much of it acquired with borrowed money. She also watched as a fire destroyed most of the new downtown business district on Christmas Day 1896. And she endured a horde of rowdy Army troops encamped in Miami during the Spanish-American War of 1898. She died unexpectedly that September at only 49 years of age. The city mourned as they interred Julia Tuttle in the new City Cemetery, outside the city limits between today's Miami and N.E. 2nd Avenues.

For her share of the settlement of the Julia Tuttle estate, her daughter Fannie—who married a Bahamian and moved to Nassau—accepted only $43,000 (equivalent to over one million 1990 dollars). Tuttle's son Harry (1870-1945), still a bachelor and living up the bay, received the remainder or bulk of the estate. He quickly married, built a fine home on the river, and began to improve his way of life. With his mother resting comfortably in the new cemetery, Harry turned her former home into a gambling casino called the Seminole Club. The club also served liquor. Julia Tuttle must have squirmed in her grave. Then he took the spacious grounds around her former home and platted a subdivision called Fort Dallas Park. This was a violation of his mother's agreement with Henry Flagler not to subdivide her home site, but the Flagler interests did not contest it. (Fort Dallas Park was not formerly subdivided until 1903.)

The boundaries of Fort Dallas Park were the grounds of the Royal Palm Hotel on the east, the spur of the railroad that ran to that hotel along the south side of today's S.E. 2nd Street on the north, and on the line of today's S.E. Miami Court on the west. Its south side bordered the Miami River. It was surrounded by a rock wall with two rock columns marking the only entrance at the foot of today's S.E. 1st Avenue. Fort Dallas Park became an elegant subdivision near the heart of the city, home to many of Miami's more prominent families. Harry E. Tuttle built the first new home there, on the largest lot, facing the central park square and extending down to the river. It was a three-story stucco house, with large open porches facing the river on the first and second

Figure 6B. The Harry E. Tuttle home with his ketch *Savalo,* **the Worthington home to the right, ca. 1910. (Historical Museum of Southern Florida)**

floors, plus a fourth floor room, perhaps for an observatory. He kept his large ketch, the *Savalo,* on the river in front of his home.

Frank T. Budge, pioneer hardware merchant, built the second new home in about 1900. It was at the southwest corner of Fort Dallas Park with 100 feet of river frontage and a depth of 240 feet. Built of the native Miami oolitic limestone, the interior was entirely native mahogany. At the southwest corner of the lot, a boat slip and house joined the river. The family lived in an apartment above the boathouse while their new home was under construction. At the north end of his deep lot, Budge built a large warehouse. Adjacent to the east of the Budge home was the home of Elizabeth Rambo, a widow from New Jersey. She had a three-and-one-half-story house with large open porches wrapping around the southeast corner. Ralph Worthington built to the east of the

Tuttle home. That house also had three-and-one-half floors; it lasted into the 1930s. Worthington's yacht *Myone*, built in 1914 and docked by his river home, was a 58-foot, "tunnel stem" boat drawing only 30 inches and powered by two Standard engines of 20 horsepower. These riverfront homes were completed by 1906. The huge Royal Palm Hotel with its beautiful grounds could be seen to the east of these homes and others in Fort Dallas Park.

The early 1920s saw a tremendous real estate boom in Miami and vicinity, with new subdivisions sprouting up everywhere and a multitude of apartment houses and hotels appearing in downtown Miami and on Miami Beach. During that four-year period, Miami's population more than doubled. Miami led the nation in construction in 1924. By that summer, on the average, each day saw the start of a new hotel or apartment building! In 1925, the pace became frantic, with much speculation in real estate. Contractors began to worry in the spring when a shortage of skilled and common labor developed, followed by a shortage of materials like Portland cement and lumber. A railroad embargo in August led to the use of old sailing vessels—mostly four-masted schooners—to transport building supplies from as far away as Canada and Europe. The boom peaked in early 1926 as the barkentine *Prins Valdemar*—the second largest vessel ever to enter Miami's harbor—sank in Government Cut, blocking all ships wishing to enter or leave.

She had been in the harbor about two months being modified as a floating hotel and cabaret. In early January, as she was being towed to her new location by the Fleetwood Hotel on Miami Beach, she ran aground and capsized in the channel. For 25 days all ship traffic stopped with some 40 ships bottled up in the harbor and almost as many waiting outside to enter and unload. A narrow channel dug around the huge ship proved unsatisfactory. That unfortunate accident broke the back of the boom. The great hurricane of September 1926 ran a dagger through its heart. By then all or part of five multi-story apartment buildings or hotels stood in Fort Dallas Park.

(It was a blessing in disguise. Without the collapse of the boom, even more of north Biscayne Bay would have been filled by artificial islands with a corresponding loss of view and natural beauty.)

On the river, the first sign of the boom came in 1918 with announcement of the Ritz-Miami Terraces. These were to be Miami's finest apartments. They were platted on the large parcel of empty land with 350 feet of river frontage that lay south of the Seminole Club ("tall building") and Fort Dallas ("long building"). The grounds of the Royal Palm Hotel were adjacent. Designed as a large H-shaped building, one long side ran along the river while the other was for a garage. There were to be 60 furnished apartments, 60 rooms for servants, 50 garages, a barber shop, beauty parlor, reception rooms, etc. Alas, it was never built.

In May 1919, $75,000 (about $1,500,000 in 1990 dollars) was paid for a riverfront lot with 200 feet of water frontage and many "tall old coconuts" that "lay considerably above the river, sloping gently to the banks of the stream." Here, a short distance west of the Royal Palm Hotel grounds, construction of the Granada Apartment Homes began in early 1922. Later known simply as the "Granada Apartments," this was Miami's first condominium apartment building. It was also the best. The "tenant ownership plan"—a collection of private homes under one roof—had already caught on in some northern cities and proved equally popular in Miami. Completed in late 1923, this C-shaped building opened toward the east (see Figure 2E). There were seven floors with 55 elegant apartment units, ranging from three rooms with one bath to seven rooms with two baths.

Figure 6C. The Granada Apartments seen from the east, ca.1923. (Matlack Collection, Historical Museum of Southern Florida)

Amenities included water softening, instantaneous garbage disposal, dry air refrigeration, electric and gas service, elevators, telephones, a community dining room and kitchen, club room, reception parlor and more. A Granada Apartments address was fashionable long after World War II—until its demolition in 1973. Today, the Hyatt Regency Hotel occupies the site; another nice place to reside, well designed and well situated on the Miami River.

The "Roaring 20s" brought excitement to the Miami River. Smuggling of contraband liquor was a thriving business. Actually, Dade County became legally "dry" in advance of the rest of the nation in 1913 when a majority of voters approved the idea in a local option election. But enforcement was impossible. The national "Prohibition Era" (1920-1933) began with ratification of the 18th Amendment to the U.S. Constitution. It was fun for the first few years, but what began as good natured disregard of the law by most parties, ended in violence and death. In the summer of 1926, a Coast Guard patrol boat and a "rum-runner" had a gun battle in front of the Granada Apartments and Grill during the dinner hour. The guardsmen fired many shots at the rum-runner's boat, whose driver crouched low in the cockpit for safety. He slipped below the Miami Avenue bridge which was too low for the patrol boat. By the time the bridge opened, after a mysterious "short delay," he got away. Mayor Sewell complained vigorously. (A grand jury investigation concluded that some Coast Guardsmen were becoming a public menace.)

On another occasion in the spring of 1929, while chasing a rum-runner near the mouth of the river, the guardsmen fired some 200 rounds of machine gun bullets, some of which hit a houseboat with people sleeping on board. Shots also hit buildings on shore. The chase continued almost to 12th Avenue, where the boat was beached with 240 sacks of booze and one bullet hole. Its occupants escaped. Rum-running and the many crimes associated with that business declined after the boom's "bust" and the onset of the Great Depression. (The "Prohibition" amendment to the Constitution was repealed in 1933.) From the 1970s into the l990s, some of the same criminal conditions exist because of the smuggling of contraband drugs, but again no solution has been found.

In 1924, Harry Tuttle had the Julia Tuttle Apartments built just west of the Granada Apartments and fronting on S.E. 4th Street—his own former home site. Architect Gordon E. Meyer designed and George Jahn built this six-story, Georgian colonial style building overlooking the river. It contained 44 apartments, 20 hotel rooms with bath and 10 rooms without bath. In the spacious lobby was a pipe organ on a raised stage, installed by the Turner Music Co. of Miami. On the top floor a sunroof overlooked the ocean, bay and river. Soon it became the Tuttle Hotel and lasted by that name until well after World War II. The Young Women's Christian Association used the building until it was torn down in the mid 1960s. Today, the Occidental Parc Suite Hotel occupies the site.

By 1924, Dr. A. O. Yearian, a retired dentist who moved to Miami from Asheville, North Carolina, in 1913, acquired the tract between the Tuttle Apartments and the Budge mansion. He built and owned the Miles Standish Hotel on the north side of downtown. Dr. Yearian announced plans to build the Miamian Hotel of 16 floors and 700 rooms here on the river. Upon learning that the Fleetwood Hotel on Miami Beach would have 16 stories, he modified his plans for a taller hotel of 20 floors and 1,000 rooms—to be the tallest in Florida! Architect C. Gault designed the building. By July, as the Tuttle Apartments neared completion, Yearian's engineers were taking ground core samples on the property and planning to move the Alhambra Apartments and Cottage across the river by barge to clear the site. (The Alhambra Apartments was the former Rambo residence and the cottage was a smaller house built on the southwest corner of the Rambo lot by the river's edge.) Dr. Yearian died unexpectedly in October while on a trip to New York. His 20-story hotel was never built. At about the same time, a million-dollar club and apartment building was announced for the Budge property, but it, too, was never built. Many dreams died with the boom's bust.

The site of the never-built Miamian Hotel became a small city park known as Fort Dallas Park. The yellow clapboard house that stands in this city park today as part of Bijan's Fort Dallas Restaurant was not originally on the river. Known as the "Palm Cottage" or "Flagler Worker's House," it was one of many such cottages built by Henry Flagler to employ and house people who were left unemployed after his Royal Palm Hotel was finished in 1897. It was moved to its present location from S.E. 2nd Street in 1980.

The new Metromover station being built (at the time of publication) just east of Miami Avenue is at another historic site. Located just outside of the Fort Dallas Park subdivision, it always had commercial use. Soon after Miami began, there was a large two-story frame building that included the Miami Fish Market and a warehouse. Newspaper articles describe it as erected in 1896 and used by J. E. Lummus for a store. An attached small brick room may have been a smokehouse. In May 1899, the "courthouse" was located on the second floor and the city government met there—above the fish house. Perhaps the small brick room served as the jail. (The court moved to a beautiful new courthouse on Flagler Street in 1904.) By 1906, the Artificial Stone Manufacturing Co. shared the property with the Miami Fish Co.

Figure 6D. The Dade County "courthouse" in the City of Miami, ca. 1900. (Florida State Archives)

This old landmark came down in 1912 to make way for a large new warehouse for the Crosland Steamship Co. which successfully introduced steamship service between Jacksonville and Miami in competition with the Florida East Coast Railway. By late summer, the name changed to the Van Steamship Co., but with John G. Crosland still in charge. In later years this company would be known simply as the "Van Line" because their steamship *Van*, built in 1914, was so often seen coming into the river. The company soon added the steamships *Dover*, *Morgan* and *Thames*. The company filled a triangular piece of river bottom to provide a planked wharf about 260 feet long. These steamships were from 190-220 feet long, 24-26 feet in beam, and drew 8-9 feet with a cargo capacity of 450-600 tons. Some ships also carried passengers. They provided regular twice weekly service between Miami and Jacksonville, as well as service to Key West. The *Thames* made the trip to Key West in 22 hours, and returned with the current in just 17 hours. The runs from Miami to Jacksonville, and the returns, took about 20 hours longer.

There was a problem caused by the rock ledge in the Miami River. As described in the first two chapters, this ledge was about half the width of the river just below Miami Avenue and tapered to a point abeam today's Bijan's Restaurant on a line with S.E. 1st Avenue. There was only some seven feet of water above the ledge, but deeper channels ran along either shore. Even in 1896, the sidewheel steamships *City of Richmond* and *City of Key West* managed to slip by the ledge to Flagler's railroad terminal dock above Miami Avenue. (There Flagler widened the river to allow for turning around.) In the fall of 1912, Crosland and the city worked jointly to remove the rock ledge that was an impediment to navigation—he at one point offering to loan the needed funds without interest because the city was "broke." They removed the rock to 11 feet except for a small portion near the line of today's S.E. 1st Avenue. The company name changed by 1915 to the Miami Steamship Co., but with Crosland still in control. For all the work done in the river and in Government Cut, no vessel of that company ever used Government Cut until 1919 (going out by Cape Florida instead)—although ships of deeper draft were reported to be using that shorter route. That August the *Thames* went out through Government Cut. (She was lost at sea off the Jupiter light in 1921.)

Crosland also ran the Miami Fish Co. during this period from the same location, plus another facility across the river. His fishing fleet consisted of 14 schooners by 1918. Queen of the fleet was the *John G. Crosland*—75 feet overall, a beam of 21 feet, and drawing four feet. Full-rigged and two-masted, she had a 60 horsepower crude oil engine, designed to stay at sea for up to a month. The *John G. Crosland* was the first company ship able to carry small boats aboard instead of in tow, and the first to have electric lights to permit working at night. About this time, the company changed its name to Miami Fisheries Co. and moved to the facility across the river west of today's Miami Avenue. (Crosland's home was nearby on today's S.W. 6th Street, to the west of 2nd Avenue.) With his fishery business doing so well, it appears that Crosland gave up control of the Miami Steamship Co.

Long a prominent citizen and leading businessman of Miami, Crosland soon made the news in a different way. The temptation of easier profits from the smuggling of liquor must have been overpowering. In August 1921, federal agents caught and arrested him while landing on the New Jersey coast with 1,000 cases of Scotch whiskey brought from Nassau. They seized the schooner *Henry L. Marshall*. On that occasion he posted a $1,000 bail bond (equivalent to about $20,000 today) and went free. Crosland was arrested again in Miami upon returning from a trip to Cuba in October. That time he turned himself in accompanied by his attorney, Redmond G. Gautier, and Congressman Frank Clark. Bail rose to $3,000 ($60,000 today) and he was charged, together with William F. McCoy and Dr. Howard Holden (a "face specialist") of Miami, with being the ring leaders of a well-organized liquor smuggling business.

Crosland fought the trial in New Jersey for over a year, through the district court in Jacksonville and the court of appeals in New Orleans, but finally was tried and convicted in New Jersey in

March 1923. The authorities in New Jersey evidently took bootlegging more seriously than some in Miami. In passing sentence, Judge Rellstab declared that Crosland was the principal conspirator in this particular case and the first of the "higher-ups" of liquor smugglers to come before him, previously seeing only "small fry." He sentenced Crosland to two years in the Atlanta penitentiary with a fine of $10,000 (equivalent to about $200,000 today). In late 1924, Bart A. Riley with some 50 businessmen and politicians petitioned newly-elected Calvin Coolidge for a presidential pardon, but without success. By then Crosland had served five months of his prison sentence, was a trustee at the penitentiary and working as prison postmaster. Probably he turned to a less risky profession after his release, although he was never mentioned in the newspapers again.

While the Crosland court action progressed, the Miami Steamship Co. purchased a big passenger liner, famous in the Klondike. The *City of Seattle*, at 257 feet, was the largest vessel ever to enter the river and proceed to the company's dock by Miami Avenue. The company dug a 15-foot deep channel for her earlier. Her skipper was Capt. W. E. Quarterman, a Miami resident for seven years. In 1922, the Clyde Steamship Co. bought the Miami Steamship Co., but it was not clear whether they would continue to operate from the river. The *Van* made her 410th and last round trip in early November 1922. Later that month the Clyde line began to operate from the municipal docks on the bayfront, dealing only in freight, although they would carry many passengers in the years to follow. In June 1924, the building formerly owned by the Miami Steamship Co. was left in ruins by an early morning fire. In November 1925, near the peak of the "boom," the Albury Co. rented the old Miami Steamship Co. dock on the river for unloading lighters from steamships.

Miami's first floating hotel was where the foot of Miami Avenue reached the north bank of the river. Capt. E. E. Vail, owner of the former steamboat *Rockledge*, towed her down to Miami shortly before the railroad arrived in 1896. She served as home to many of Miami's prominent early citizens. She began life in 1859 as the *Governor Jonathan Worth*, named after the governor of North Carolina where she plied the Cape Fear River as far as Fayetteville. At 150 feet with twin sidewheels, she was one of the largest and fastest of her type. Captured by General Sherman, she served the Union forces during the Civil War. After the war she became the *Rockledge*. Among her celebrated passengers were President and Mrs. Grover Cleveland on their honeymoon voyage to Florida. Vail bought her afterward, but soon found her boilers unfit. He turned her into a floating hotel and towed her to West Palm Beach, later following Flagler south to Miami.

In her old age, the *Rockledge* served as a gambling hall. In 1901, U.S. Marshall Charles J. Rose (later in the cement block business) raided the *Rockledge* to find a complete moonshiner's still and a bushel basket full of poker chips. Later, with her sides boarded up, she became an "assignation house" or brothel—still by Miami Avenue but west on the south shore. In November 1913, with a large crowd watching, some men with tears in their eyes, she was towed three miles out to sea and sunk as the first of the area's artificial reefs.

On the South Side of the River

The south side of the river in this stretch was always commercial. In contrast to the beautiful grounds of the Brickell estate east of the line of today's Brickell Avenue, here west of the avenue the plants of the Standard Oil Co. and the Gulf Oil Co. were situated. The former probably came after 1903 when the Miami Avenue bridge opened. The latter came in 1908. Both companies sold gasoline, kerosene, lubricating oils and such products. Both had piers extending into the river and large storage tanks on shore. By 1913, a fire adjacent to these properties caused south-side citizens to petition for their removal to a different location. However, the Standard Oil Co. plant lasted into the early 1930s, and the Gulf Oil Co. plant remained in some form until the mid-1930s. The Rivergate Plaza and the U. S. Customs building occupy the sites today.

Next to the west, W. J. Huffstetler came from West Palm Beach in 1906 to build a boat yard just east of where the south shore bulges northward even today. It was a large facility with two marine railways where boats were built as well as serviced. In late 1909, Huffstetler built a 55-foot canopied launch which he intended to operate himself in the tourist passenger business up the river and the new Miami Canal where the dredge was excavating. (The venture did not last long. For some months one could motor four miles or more up the new canal, but by mid-1910, a temporary dam was installed about three miles above the junction of the Miami Canal with the Miami River.) In 1912, Huffstetler sold his old yard and took over the Miami Yacht and Machine Works Co., just upstream by today's Miami Avenue bridge. The new owner of Huffstetler's old yard suffered a misfortune in May 1913 when the fire mentioned above destroyed the yard.

Abijan H. Pelsang, who at one time had four boat yards on the Miami River (see Chapters 8, 9, and 12), acquired Huffstetler's old yard later. He ran this yard at least through 1921, adding a third marine railway. Boat craftsman Tommy Curry once worked for Pelsang, perhaps in this very yard, although the yard became a vacant lot well before the 1920s ended.

In 1929, Charles and Tommy Curry established Tommy's Boat Yard at this location. The Curry brothers came to Miami in the mid-1910s from Harbor Island in the Bahama Islands. They had been coming over on their father's schooner since 1905. On land leased from George Brickell, they dug a slip and put in a bulkhead. Charlie ran the office and Tommy, who had previous boat yard experience, ran the yard. There were about 14 employees during the early years. Despite the Great Depression, they prospered repairing the yachts of the rich and famous, and for a while, the boats of rum-runners. Gar Wood, Errol Flynn, Charles Kettering and Lana Turner, among other celebrities, all took their yachts to Tommy's. A few boats were built during the slower summer months.

After the 1935 hurricane, repair of damaged boats, including those of Roddey Burdine and Hugh Matheson, helped get the Currys on their feet. They acquired more land, added more railway, a new shop and new machinery. During World War II, the yard was conscripted for repair of Navy and Coast Guard boats up to 57 feet. Others up to 300 feet were repaired in the river. Most of the work involved installing depth chargers and gun turrets, and they did it on a contract basis. Charles's son Bo took over the yard during the war. After the war, the trade evolved to middle class people with smaller boats. During the 1970s, repair of boats for smuggling hard drugs took the place once filled by the boats of rum-runners. It was a very personal, one-family operation. By the early 1980s, taxes in excess of $30,000 per year were threatening to put Tommy's out of business soon. Their lease ran out in 1985, but Tommy's Boat Yard did not close until April 1986. Today, there is only a large vacant lot and an empty slip adjacent to the U.S. Customs building.

Just west of the line of S.E. 1st Avenue where the south shore bulges north—where Dr. Fletcher had his store from 1844 to 1870—was the Benner Sail Line (also known as the Benner Schooner Line). The company was 60 years old with offices in many ports of the world, including Tampa, when it established a branch here on the river in 1905. Their wharf was 50 feet wide by 150 feet long, from which schooners like the *Edith* and *May* sailed regularly to New York. Capt. William Burch, who later retired in Miami (see Chapter 18) commanded the *Edith* and *May*. The Benner Line, with schooners, was the first to offer competition to the Florida East Coast Railway. The company represented other lines to Central America.

There was much schooner traffic between the Bahama Islands and Miami that came and went from either the Benner Line dock or later "Cook's Dock." Memorable ship names included the *Fearless, Hattie Darling, Olivette* and the *William H. Albury*. Thousands of black Bahamians came over the years, many of them to work in the groves or farms during the "cropping" season. Many stayed to make their homes in Miami, and some prospered. In those years, blacks from the Bahamas tended to consider themselves as almost social equals to white people in Miami. It was an idea they had to abandon upon arrival or find life very difficult, even dangerous or fatal. Fortunately, many were able to adjust.

The "Benner Dock" became "Cook's Dock" with 220 feet of river frontage in 1909 although many continued to use the old name. A Canadian by birth, George F. Cook worked in various parts of Canada and the northern United States before landing in New York where he manufactured a breakfast food called "Cook's Flake Rice." He first came to Miami in 1903, sailing with one son on their boat *Zora* to visit another son. The warm climate impressed him and he soon returned for his health.

Cook built jetties, seawalls and other contract work for several years. He and one of six sons were living on a houseboat they built when his wife and youngest son arrived from New York to join them just before the hurricane of 1906. Tied at the Royal Palm Hotel pier, both houseboat and pier were torn away during the storm. (This hurricane passed directly over Miami with the calm of the eye lasting 30 minutes.) The telegram announcing Mrs. Cook's coming was delivered 14 hours after her arrival. She moved ashore with pleasure to a "regular" house where they could also keep a black goat and a flock of white chickens.

George F. Cook with E. E. Phelps organized the Cook Steamship Co. in 1909. Cook ran the first independent steamship to bring freight into Miami, a small steamer aptly named the *Magic City*. Like the Benner Line schooners, it competed with the Florida East Coast Railway and offered lower rates. But the *Magic City* was short lived, sinking in the St. Johns River the following year,

Figure 6E. Schooners near Cook's Dock, ca. 1910. (Historical Museum of Southern Florida)

perhaps the result of foul play. The Cook Co. was an odd one in that they also ran schooners with freight to Key West and charters for passengers to foreign places. In Key West freight could be put on faster ships bound for New York and other northern ports, in that way competing with the railroad. In addition, the company advertised towing and lighterage, ship's brokers, and dealing in cement, coal oil, sand and other commodities. "Cook's Dock" was a popular stopping place for boats from the Bahamas.

Cook's Dock appears to have been sold to the L. T. Highleymans by 1913 who sold in that year to McLendon, Keller and Keller who planned to manufacture ice. (Cook may have caught the real estate fever. By the late 1910s he was an officer of the Chevelier Corporation, a group promoting a planned new town on the Tamiami Trail then under construction.) By 1918, the Florida Key Lime Co. occupied the dock site, a fruit packing business sharing space with a fishery. During the period 1920-23, the Waldeck-Deal Dredging Co. used the dock (see Chapter 12).

The Warriner-DesRocher Machine Shop occupied this site from the late 1920s into the 1990s. Arthur DesRocher came to Miami in about 1910. He worked for the Miami Yacht and Machine Works in the 1910s, and in the early 1920s had a machine shop with G. A. Freas on the south shore west of Miami Avenue. Alfred F. Warriner arrived in about 1920 and worked for the Bowers-Southern and Clark Dredging Cos. Together, Warriner and DesRocher founded one of the largest machine shops on the river that served its users for well over half a century.

The Miami Boat Works was the oldest yard of its kind on the river, established by Peck and Bailey sometime before 1904—probably in 1903 after the Miami Avenue bridge opened. Located just east of Miami Avenue, it was on part of Dr. Fletcher's 19th century property. They built boats, had a marine railway, and dealt in sails, engines, etc. Their most famous customer was, without doubt, Captain Joshua Slocum, whose 40-foot yacht *Spray* is shown on their ways in 1908. (For the non-sailor, Capt. Slocum became famous when he took his little ship single-handed around the

Figure 6F. Captain Joshua Slocum's famous yacht *Spray* at the Miami Boat Works, 1908. (Historical Museum of Southern Florida)

world in the 1890s. He was on that voyage when the City of Miami began.) He may have visited Miami in the spring of 1906 and 1907, while returning from trips to the Caribbean, and certainly was on the Miami River in January 1908 when he met Vincent Gilpen (co-author of *The Commodore's Story*). Captain Slocum was 64 years old then, and died at sea the following year.

Under new management, the Miami Boat Works became the Miami Yacht and Machine Co. in late 1908. It was this yard that W. I. Huffstetler came upstream to run in 1912. Huffstetler greatly improved the yard by dredging a canal 200 feet long with a marine railway able to lift a boat of 800 tons. Large vessels previously required to go to Jacksonville or Tampa for service began to come to Huffstetler's new yard. Huffsterler added even greater capacity in 1913, and again in 1914. The yard came to include six marine railways with tracks and cradles, one large two-story building and several smaller ones for shops, storage, etc. Boats were built as well as serviced.

One of the first boats built at Huffstetler's new facility was the famous *Blue Dog*, a houseboat described as a "floating palace." Paul Chalfin, the very cultivated gentleman engaged by James Deering to oversee the construction and furnishing of his Villa Vizcaya, had it built in 1915. The *Blue Dog* was 74 feet long by 24 feet wide with two decks. The main salon had a 10-foot ceiling with chandeliers and a big stone fireplace. Cypress slabs three feet wide paneled the interior walls. Awnings and window boxes adorned 10 windows along each side. There were three staterooms for Chalfin and his guests and three other rooms for servants—the service and kitchen part of the boat being entirely separate. At each end was a 10 by 24 foot screened porch. The entire top deck was canopied. Beautifully furnished, the *Blue Dog* became a sensation and set an example for others who could afford such things.

Paul Chalfin docked his *Blue Dog* variously on the bayfront, at Carl Fisher's place on Miami Beach and on the Miami River. A Mr. Gattis bought her later. In October 1921, a hurricane alert

Figure 6G. Paul Chalfin's houseboat *Blue Dog*, ca. 1917. (Historical Museum of Southern Florida)

caused her to be towed upriver to Grove Park, just below 17th Avenue. About midnight she broke away from her mooring as a squall swept up the river and an unexplained fire broke out. The fire department, which arrived late on the wrong side of the river, reported that no one was aboard at the time. She burned to the water before anything could be done.

Huffstetler's Miami Yacht and Machine Co. was gone by the late 1930s. During the 1940s and 1950s, non-water-dependent businesses occupied the site.

From the beginning of the city, many people lived aboard houseboats on the Miami River and Biscayne Bay. They ran the gamut of those who simply preferred that way of life to millionaires who had veritable floating mansions. A newspaper feature in 1923 described "Miami's Houseboat Colony." The *Blue Dog*, pictured above, was listed as No. 1. No. 2 was a family houseboat in the upper reaches of the river. No. 3 was a large houseboat with an avenue of royal palms leading to its gangway. No. 4, *Snug Harbor*, was in a cozy harbor at Harry Tuttle's place in Fort Dallas Park. No. 5, actually a group of smaller houseboats, was among some 50 of the type on the north shore above Flagler Street. No. 6, *Silver Moon*, was in the bay, perhaps to better observe the moon rising. No. 7 also was at Fort Dallas Park, but unnamed. Finally, No. 8, the *Kewah*, was noted earlier as belonging to Capt. Tom Newman and kept at his pier on the bayshore before Bayfront Park began. Formerly a charter fishing boat, the Ted Housers occupied it, still in the bay. Another former houseboat shown was no longer a home. Quite large and elaborate with two decks, it became a floating restaurant and dance pavilion. During the 1930s, the *Miami Daily News* publishing company maintained a cruising houseboat with twin decks for the use of its employees or company guests. Whether essential or for pleasure, houseboats have always been a part of the river scene.

Figure 6H. Original 1903 Miami Avenue bridge, ca. 1910. (Historical Museum of Southern Florida)

A ferry operated by the Brickells once crossed the river. As mentioned previously, the first bridge to cross the Miami River was a crude affair at Avenue G, today's S.W. 2nd Avenue, about half a mile upstream from the bay and a substantial bridge did not cross the river until 1903.

In 1901, the County Commission had approved this new steel bridge to replace the old wooden drawbridge that was becoming unsafe. The bridge location was moved to Avenue D, today's Miami Avenue. During its construction, John Sewell discovered a subterranean stream or spring on the river bottom in some 14 feet of depth. The design of that first bridge was modified to avoid the mouth of this spring or underground stream. It opened to the public in August 1903 as a manually operated swing bridge of steel and wood with two lanes for vehicles and a pedestrian walkway, turning on a masonry pedestal in the center of the river. The bridge tender would insert a long steel crank, then, sometimes assisted by a small boy, walk it around and around to rotate the long bridge span until parallel with the navigation channels. Then marine traffic could pass through channels on either side. Protective devices were almost nil and at least one Miami motorist drove off into the river while the bridge was turned.

Figure 61. Bridge tender with boy assistant turning the old Miami Avenue swing bridge, ca. 1917. (Miami News Collection, Historical Museum of Southern Florida)

The city authorized a new bridge to cross the river on Miami Avenue in 1915. By then, the "substantial" swing bridge, barely a dozen years old, was rusting and considered dangerous. Harrington, Howard and Ash of Kansas City, Missouri, designed the second bridge. The M. F. Comer Co. of Miami built it. They installed the old span temporarily just upstream the following summer. Construction was delayed partly because clean white sand was difficult to obtain, it having been covered in the bay by muck from digging the Miami Canal. It was delayed also because the bridge architects failed to avoid the mouth of the subterranean stream or spring found in building the original bridge. Three days before the new bridge opened in March 1918, the old bridge broke beneath a truck. The new bridge was of the bascule type with four lanes, built of steel and concrete, and electrically-powered. It lasted until 1979—61 years of faithful service.

For several years there was no crossing at Miami Avenue while construction of a modern, hydraulically-powered, bascule bridge of six lanes was underway. It opened in 1986, and has separate north-bound and south-bound sections of three lanes each, the bascule supporting structures staggered to match the angle at which the avenue crosses the river here. Historically, motorists complained of how slowly the older bridge opened. The situation appears little improved with this new bridge. Its longevity remains to be determined.

The new Miami Avenue bridge is painted pale yellow in accordance with the "rainbow plan" sponsored by the Miami River Coordinating Committee in 1985.

Chapter 7
Miami Avenue to S.W. 2ⁿᵈ Avenue

The land on the north shore of the river immediately west of Miami Avenue served a variety of purposes. Henry Flagler dredged some of it out originally to accommodate the sidewheel steamship *City of Richmond* that was 225 feet long, 50 feet in beam and drew 7-1/2 feet. (Chapter 2 mentioned how he made a 60-foot wide channel for her.) Over the years, this site appears to have been filled in and dredged out more than once. The J. C. Rose Concrete and Artificial Stone Co. occupied the site during the first decade of the 20th century. Several fisheries occupied the site just to the west during those early years.

The Southern Utilities Co. was making extensive improvements at this site by 1914 and went into the fishery business. Their wharf extended east to the Avenue D (today's Miami Avenue) bridge. The City Ice and Cold Storage Co. was behind their plant. Ice was essential for all the fisheries along the river.

In about 1920, the I. E. Schilling Co. relocated next to the Southern Utilities Co. from an earlier site about half a mile upstream that they occupied for some six years. Schilling was another of those early Miamians who came here originally for his health and decided to stay. He had a steamship business in Greenbay, Wisconsin, where his company handled much Portland cement. Seeing the need for building materials in Miami, he moved south in 1912 and soon was providing most of the materials for homes and buildings in Miami. His company operated three yards with 10 motor trucks, 50 mules, 10 barges, and 8 tug boats. In 1924, he bought the adjacent Southern Utilities Co. property, then expanded his yard with 500 feet of river frontage, a boat yard to service his barges and tug boats, sand and stone hoppers, a railroad spur, etc. He continued to operate his other two yards upriver. At the peak of the 1920s building boom, he had five yards. The company's main yard was in that riverside location into the 1940s. Schilling was secretary-treasurer of the Belcher Asphalt Co. that became the Belcher Oil Co. (today's Coastal Fuel), served as a director of the First National Bank and the Chamber of Commerce, and was active in civic groups until his death in 1931.

Along the line of today's Metrorail, midway between today's Miami and S.W. 2nd Avenues, Henry Flagler brought his Florida East Coast Railway to the north bank of the Miami River in April 1896. His railroad terminal dock on the river was here to the east side. That May the sidewheel steamship *City of Key West* began regular service between Miami and Key West. She departed Miami on Tuesday, Thursday and Saturday, and returned on Monday, Wednesday and Friday, making connections with the F.E.C. Railway trains from Jacksonville. Other steamships also used the river terminal dock, sailing to Nassau or Jacksonville. Within a year Flagler built another terminal dock on the bay at 6th Street. (Sixth Street is the only street to have the same number under the original street numbering system and the subsequent system adopted in January 1921, still in use today.) This steamer traffic gradually moved to the bayshore terminal dock. While Flagler was building his "Overseas Extension" of the Florida East Coast Railway to Key West, after 1905, there was heavy marine traffic from the river terminal dock transporting a mass of construction materials to the Florida Keys.

Figure 7A. Sidewheel steamship *City of Key West* leaving the Miami River, ca. 1897. (Historical Museum of Southern Florida)

One should note that the City of Miami did not develop because it had a good deep water port—it did not—but rather because of the railroad. Today's deep water port in Biscayne Bay was built by dredging.

Adjacent to the west of the railroad originally was the Florida East Coast Electric Light and Waterworks Plant. Adjacent to the east was a large F.E.C. Railway freight house. By 1910, a second freight house was built. These were long buildings parallel to the tracks. By 1914, six railroad tracks ran to the river's edge east of the main line, and a deep boat slip lay west of it. The electric light and waterworks facility became the Miami Electric Light & Power Co., Inc., together with the Miami Water Co., Inc. The water works were soon gone. By the 1920s, both the boat slip and the freight houses were greatly enlarged. The large freight house stood into the 1980s.

Flagler's Florida East Coast Railway crossed the Miami River headed south to Homestead in 1903. There is reason to believe that Flagler delayed this continuation of his railroad until convinced that the United States would build an inter-ocean canal in Panama. The Congress approved purchase of the French canal property in Panama in June 1902, and President Theodore Roosevelt aided the formation of the Republic of Panama the following year. Key West was the closest American port to Panama. The advantages of a steamship-railroad connection were obvious. Construction of the Panama Canal and Flagler's Overseas Extension of his railroad to Key West took place at about the same time—both were engineering marvels of the day.

The F.E.C. Railway built a swing-type, single-track railroad bridge that was initially manually operated. It rotated on a massive central pedestal with marine traffic passing through 50 foot wide channels on either side. After the new Miami Avenue bridge was completed in 1918, the city tried unsuccessfully to have the F.E.C. Railway enlarge their bridge to provide 75-foot wide channels on either side while the company installed a replacement bridge. Probably the bridge was electrically powered at that time. As the Corps of Engineers began the deepening and widening of the Miami River in 1932, Miami citizens petitioned for 75-foot wide navigation channels. A longer railroad bridge was built in 1933, and the piers were strengthened. (See Figure 7C.) Destruction of the Overseas Extension of the railroad in the great "Labor Day Hurricane" of 1935 greatly reduced train traffic across the river. There was an increase during World War II. A dramatic event took place in 1962—the year of the famous "Cuban Missile Crisis"—involving the southward passage of many trains carrying Army Nike missile batteries and a mass of other military equipment to defend South Florida from the threat of Soviet missiles installed in Cuba.

With trains no longer running south, the old swing bridge was removed in 1969, but the massive central support pedestal remained in the river until 1978. Probably this obstruction to large ships passing delayed the development of the Miami Canal above 27th Avenue as a major port.

Metrorail crosses the river today on the old F.E.C. Railway right-of-way. This electric commuter train, with twin tracks on a high fixed bridge, began service in 1984. It blocked the passage of tall-masted ships upstream to the Interstate-95 expressway and the Miami Shipyards Corporation by the S.W. 2nd Avenue bridge (see below).

Mostly vacant land occupied the north shore of the river to the west of the F.E.C. Railway and related facilities, until the mid-1920s. In late 1925, the City Curb Market rose here. Voters approved a bond issue to relocate an older market in new buildings, operated under the supervision of the city. It was a boon to housewives and others as farmers from four counties brought fresh produce to sell. Two beautiful long open buildings running parallel to the river had long open sides and red tile roofs supported by concrete columns. These were for farm products. Closer to the river's edge was a smaller fish market building of similar design. There was a small dock next to S.W. 2nd Avenue. (See Figure 7C.) The Curb Market was extensively remodeled in 1936, continuing popular through that decade. In about 1940, the fish market building became the City Jail. The City Curb Market was taken over during World War II by the Miami Shipbuilding Corporation (see below). After the war, this beautiful complex was used for such mundane activities as automobile repairs. Today, a substation of the Florida Power and Light Co. occupies the site.

On the South Side of the River

Mostly small businesses occupied the south shore just west of today's Miami Avenue in the early years. These included the L. E. Bunnel machine shop founded by brothers Luther and Otis Bunnell in 1911, and the Miami Tent and Awning Co. that made boat awnings. In the 1920s, Curry's Fish Market and Thos. Fenwick, dealing in wholesale fish sales, were located here.

Next to the west, at 51 S.W. Miami Avenue Road, George A. Freas and Arthur DesRocher had a machine shop in the early 1920s. DesRocher was manager as well as machinist, while Freas served also as secretary-treasurer. Both men had lived in Miami at least a decade and probably were old friends. In the last chapter we saw that DesRocher joined with Warriner in a larger machine shop downstream in the late 1920s. That is when Freas retired (see Chapter 11). Dawson's Marine service station occupies part of this property today.

A fruit packing plant with a long planked wharf was located adjacent to the west by 1910 where the Big Fish Restaurant is today. From 1914 to 1921 this became the Fish House. Until after World War II, an automobile filling station and repair shop occupied the site.

John Crosland's Miami Fish Co. with a long wharf and its own ice plant was adjacent to the railroad (today's Metrorail) on the east, from at least 1914 (see Chapter 6). In 1918, the name changed to Miami Fisheries Co. as Crosland consolidated that business at this location only. It continued through the 1920s. By the end of World War II, there was only an ice plant. Some say that an illegal bolita operation ran from the ice house afterward.

As noted previously, the Florida East Coast Railway crossed the river in 1903 on the line of today's Metrorail. Here on the south shore by the west side of the tracks was the bridgetender's house (see Figure 7C). It was two stories with gables in a Bermuda roof, painted "Flagler yellow" with white trim. When a train approached to cross the river, the bridgetender would receive a telegraph message to alert him. He then jumped into his skiff and rowed out to the bridge, securing the skiff on the downflow end, and crawling aboard to rotate the bridge. By the 1920s, the bridge was electrically powered and his control station sat on a corner of the bridge. Heavy steel walls formed the sides, so that any locomotive or train car that might jump the track would not land in the river. Some still remember a well known bridgetender, "Herndon," from the 1920s and 1930s.

❧❦

Between the railroad and Avenue G (today's S.W. 2nd Avenue), where the river makes a bend and reaches its most southern extent, C. E. Thomson wrote that the Indians used to beach their dugout canoes while trading at Brickell's store—at the point where the river meets the bay, about half a mile downstream. By the end of 1896, C. C. Cutrell had a boat yard with marine railway on the south shore of the river "near the bridge". Since there was then only the Avenue G bridge, and the yard probably was on the downstream side, it must have been located here. As early as 1906, the K. M. Large & Co. boat storage and repair with two small ways occupied the site, adding a marine railway later. In 1907, A. Jafredsen built a sail loft above Capt. Large's shed and they worked together.

Capt. S. Gedney bought this property in 1911, and in about 1917 turned it over to his brother-in-law, Morton Fogal. Fogal was a sailmaker and boatbuilder whose family had been in the boat building business on the east coast since 1824, having started on Long Island Sound. In winter he catered to visiting yachtsmen, steadily increasing in number, and during the hot summer months he served the commercial boatmen and built boats for the following winter season. In 1921, S.W. 6th Street was platted along the south shore of the river through a small concrete block building, three of Fogal's marine railways, and his sail loft, to join S.W. 1st Avenue. (The bridge at S.W. 2nd Avenue was authorized in 1915, but construction did not begin until 1923.)

In 1922, the Fogal Boat Yard advertised adding two more marine railways, with roller bearing cradles on solid rock foundations, and powerful electric drive motors—and being within a 10-minute walk from the post office. (Evidently the railways were not added, because Fogal continued with only three.) Lighter houseboats with city water and electrical connections received the same service without charge while on the ways. Superintendent Henry L. Russell was a graduate of the Mathis Boat Building Co. of New Jersey, and had been in charge of the Murdock Ship Yard in Jacksonville during World War I. Forty men were regularly employed, with half again that many during the winter months. Fogal built a great many boats of all sizes in his yard. In 1923, he built an 85-foot Glouster-type fishing boat for a man in New Jersey. They advertised being able to design and build boats of any size. The yard continued to prosper into the 1930s. Some say that during the Prohibition Era, Fogal's yard built powerful boats for rum-runners side-by-side with similar boats built for the Coast Guard.

Adjacent to the line of S.W. 2nd Avenue, R. I. Jeffords built a machine shop in 1908. In 1914, there was a machine and electric motor shop with a planked wharf that ran along the shore below today's bridge to join a boat yard adjacent on the west side. This became the Lyne Riverside Machine Shop in 1918. Jeffords joined with T. P. Way, another machinist, to form the Jeffords-Way Machine Co. in about 1920.

Morton Fogal died in 1935. Emil Buhler, with three sons, P.H., T.C., and Jean E. Buhler, bought the Fogal Boat Yard and the Jeffords-Way Machine Co. and continued operations under the Fogal name. In 1937, they built a large marine railway that could haul 750 tons. It was at an acute angle to the river and located on the site of the former Jeffords-Way Machine Co., next to S.W. 2nd Avenue. Another marine railway was built on the east side of the property. Various jobs brought

Figure 7B. The Fogal Boat Yard, 1937. (Historical Museum of Southern Florida)

Figure 7C. Miami Shipbuilding Corp., looking north, 1941. PT-1 and PT-2 are seen in the lower right. Also note the F.E.C. Railway Co.'s railroad bridge tender's house to the right, and the City Curb Market north of the river on the left. (Jean E. Buhler)

prosperity and expansion, so in 1939 they changed the name to Miami Shipbuilding Corporation (MSC). That company became very active during World War II.

The MSC bid for construction of the first PT (patrol torpedo) boats for the U.S. Navy in 1939, and won a contract to build PT-l and PT-2. George F. Crouch, reknowned naval architect, designed these boats in a competition. They were powerful 59-foot boats, built here on the river. A clause in the bid contract proved both fortunate and very profitable. The PT boat contract provided for a $500 per day penalty if the boats were not delivered on time. It also provided for a $500 per day penalty on the Government if the engines were not provided on time. Those specially built "Vimalert" engines for PT-l and PT-2 were provided 31 months late! (Because of that delay, PT-l and PT-2 did not enter active service until later model PTs were built and deployed—not until after the United States had entered the war.) Before those special engines were delivered, the MSC improved the original PT design for a 63-foot Aircraft Rescue Boat (ARB) that was even faster; powered by 650 horsepower engines. (Air Rescue Boats are used to rescue downed pilots, not aircraft.) The MSC built 327 of those ARBs for the United States and various foreign governments. They built one ARB in just 18 days—from laying the keel to launching and its U.S. Navy sea trial! These boats served widely in the Mediterranean Sea and Pacific Ocean theaters of operation. And they served in many capacities other than aircraft pilot rescues.

Figure 7D. PT-2 on sea trials off Miami Beach, 1942. (Historical Museum of Southern Florida)

In addition to the 63-foot Air Rescue Boats, the MSC built six 30-foot and two 34-foot coastal patrol boats for the Dutch government, plus other boats for other countries. They also converted many kinds of private boats for use by the U.S. Navy and Coast Guard. These were boats or ships from 38 to 170 feet long.

Along with the MSC's main yard on the river, they had several others working in support of the same effort. Boats launched on the river were completed in a yard at the foot of Aviation Avenue in Coconut Grove, where Monty Trainer's restaurant is today. It could handle five boats abreast in the water. They ran the Seaboard Lumber Yard (today's Gancedo's Lumber Yard) at N.W. 17th Avenue and 20th Street, and the Coral Gables Lumber Yard at San Lorenzo and Ponce de Leon west of the railroad spur. There was a foundry on Mundy Street and Dixie Highway in Coconut Grove. A plating plant was at N.W. 5th Street near the bridge, and a tin shop on S.W. 6th Street near the main plant. The MSC acquired the Beach Boat Slips in Miami Beach for non-military work. The City Curb Market across the river next to S.W. 2nd Avenue was used for prefabricating parts. The former Ryan Building (a Ford, Lincoln, & Mercury agency) nearby on North River Drive was purchased as a warehouse for storing parts and making up boat building "kits." At the time of peak production in 1943, there were 1,800 employees. The MSC achieved a production peak of one boat per working day. This wartime production won the company an Army/Navy "E" for excellence with five stars (repeat awards).

An interesting anecdote from that period relates to the "midgets." The Ringling Brothers Circus shut down during the war. A group of Russian midgets was stranded in South Florida and wanted to contribute to the war effort. They came to Miami where the MSC hired them to install wiring and perform other jobs inside the boats. Most of these midgets lived in the Village of Sweetwater where they were among the founding fathers. Two had small scale houses built adjacent to St. Vladimir Russian Orthodox Church in Exile, off Flagler Street, where they were very active members of the congregation. Those two small houses were donated to the church which enabled it to survive some difficult times. Several houses of seven-eighths scale were built for these midgets along Miller Drive near 62nd Avenue and are there today. The last of these midgets, well loved by those who knew her, passed on in 1976 at the age of 83.

During the 1950s, the MSC helped pioneer the design and manufacture of hydrofoils. They also built many shrimpers and promoted the "trawler hull" design before it became popular in private yachts. Perhaps they were ahead of their time and invested too much in those efforts.

The MSC property was going into bankruptcy in 1960 when it was acquired by a real estate investment firm of Washington, D.C. James W. Brown came down from Washington to examine the property in 1965. The name had just been changed to the Miami Shipyards Corporation. Brown initially meant to sell the property, but learning that the Dade Drydock Co. (formerly at the old Port of Miami) was about to leave the area, he realized the opportunity for a successful shipyard here. The three marine railways were a great asset, but the buildings were in disrepair and the tugs and other equipment were scattered or missing. He began immediately to improve the yard. A distinguishing feature of that property today, as it was when built by the Miami Shipbuilding Corporation in 1943, is the two-story art deco style administration building. It is recognized by many people around the world as the "police headquarters" from the "Miami Vice" television series of the 1980s when it was often used as a prop.

The new Miami Shipyards Corporation began servicing island boats, such as Bahamian freighters and the Bahamian mail boat. Soon they began to service larger vessels. Today they service, among others, ships of the U.S. Air Force Jump School at Homestead Air Force Base and large Coast Guard cutters. In 1992, it is one of the largest shipyards on the east coast south of Jacksonville.

Figure 7E. Miami Shipyards Corporation's art deco administration building, 1990. (Irene Y. Purdy)

Besides the shipyard proper, the corporation includes Miami Ships Services, which is an agent for the Betty K Line of Nassau. The *Betty K* is regularly seen at their seawall.

In 1896, Flagler's people built the very first bridge to cross the river—here on Avenue G, today's S.W. 2nd Avenue. Two early Miami merchants, J. W. Johnson and Isidor Cohen, opened stores on the south bank in anticipation of that first bridge. John Sewell wrote that it was a "wooden bridge with a sliding draw and an apron on one end where the draw ran back on the stationary part of the bridge. When the draw was going to be opened, this long apron was raised and the bridge would be moved with a cog wheel and lever . . . ." It was a "poor apology for a bridge," and today one may wonder whether Flagler himself was aware of the poor design. It lasted until 1902 or 1903, but was considered unsafe toward the end.

For two decades, from 1903 (when the Miami Avenue bridge opened) until 1924, this location was without a bridge. In 1915, a bridge at today's S.W. 2nd Avenue was proposed to serve temporarily while the Miami Avenue and Flagler Street bridges were being replaced. A bond issue passed that year provided the needed funds, and by June 1917 the design plans were completed. It would be a bascule type bridge, but lighter than the others because no trolley line was anticipated. (Today it is the only bridge of only two lanes to cross the river.) Increasing costs and insufficient funds, coupled with the difficulty of securing materials during wartime, delayed construction. Also, a change in plans called for making it stronger to support a trolley line. The War Department (today referred to as the Army Corps of Engineers) finally gave its approval in 1920, but red tape, additional plan changes and funding difficulties brought more delays. In August 1922, the Comer-Ebsary Foundation Co. (see Chapter 16) won the contract for construction. It was to have a span of 115 feet, nine feet of vertical clearance when closed and provide for a trolley. The plan called for a boat landing and nice plantings at the north end. The new bridge opened in April 1924, making it the second oldest working bridge on the river system at 68 years old. It provided many business and residential opportunities on the south side of the river in that area.

In the early 1990s, a new bridge was being designed for the S.W. 2nd Avenue location that will have four lanes and hydraulic power. It will have 26 feet of vertical clearance and 90 feet of horizontal clearance with the spans open. Start of construction is scheduled for 1995. The Miami River Coordinating Committee's "rainbow plan" color for this bridge is a bright yellow.

Chapter 8
S.W. 2nd Avenue to Flagler Street

During the 1920s and 1930s, a property of Hugh M. Matheson stood on the present site of the stark marble edifice of the Florida Power and Light Co. on the north shore adjacent to S.W. 2nd Avenue. Hugh was a son of William J. Matheson who built a palatial home on Key Biscayne. Here on the river he had a beautiful three-story office building, boat shop and a dock from which employees and supplies were ferried to the estate on Key Biscayne. On New Year's Day of 1931, having just moved upriver (see Chapter 4), the spacious third floor of the Matheson building became the temporary home of the Biscayne Bay Yacht Club. The yacht club met in these elegant quarters until their new clubhouse was completed in Coconut Grove in mid-1932.

Figure 8A. Matheson Office Building, ca. 1931. (Hardy Matheson and Historical Museum of Southern Florida)

On the small triangular parcel of land just west of the S.W. 2nd Avenue bridge that includes a small boat slip and larger double boat slip, a boat yard and the tall tower of radio station WWPG were located through the 1970s. Today, this parcel is part of the Florida Power and Light Co. property mentioned above.

To the west, about where the Interstate-95 expressway crosses the river, in 1912 the Furst-Clark Construction Co. built an office and facilities for the repair and servicing of their dredges and barges. The company won the contract in 1910 for completing the state's Miami Canal (see Chapter 3). That major project was completed in 1913, but the company remained in Miami to do many other dredge and fill projects. Robert P. Clark was president and had a home in Miami because so much of the firm's work was done in this area. This company was later absorbed by the Bowers-Southern Dredging Co.

In 1917, Bowers-Southern won a contract to widen and deepen part of the Miami Canal (which Furst-Clark had never completed to specifications earlier). For this project they used the *Governor Herrick* (see Figure 2C), one of the largest dipper dredges ever built with a bucket taking up to 10 cubic yards with each dip. It had its own power and refrigerating plants, and complete facilities for housing, feeding and caring for a crew of 40 men. Other company dredges used in the Miami area were the *Miami*, the *Biscayne* and the *Florida*. Also at this location through the 1930s were the Arundel Corp., the Megathlin & Clark Dredging Co., and the Clark Dredging Co., all of which were active in the boom years of Miami's development. In the early 1930s, the Clark Dredging Co. had a subcontract from the Standard Dredging Co. to deepen and widen the Miami River and Canal for the Army Corps of Engineers, because the prime contractor was too small to do the job. Their dredge *Arundel* worked down from the northwest end of the stream while their huge dredge *Norman H. Davis* (see Figure 2D) worked up from the mouth of the river on this mammoth excavation.

Elsewhere along the north shore from the 1910s through the 1930s were a number of boat yards and fish houses, the Miami Outboard Motor & Boat Co., and the Atlas Rock Co., located across the river from today's Jose Marti Park. John Deer and his son, J. M. Deer, president and secretary-treasurer, respectively, took over the Atlas Rock Co. in 1922. Their business doubled in 1924 as Miami's building boom neared its peak. They dealt in sand, rock, lime, plaster, cement, sewer pipe, clay products, reinforcing and structural steel. Their 160 feet of river frontage was an advantage. Along with barges, they operated 12 trucks for landslide deliveries.

On the north shore 90 feet east of the old Twelfth Street bridge (today's Flagler Street bridge), E. H. Lyon of New York built the Lyon wharf in 1911, adding 200 feet of river dockage. A well known manufacturer of Lyon's Tooth Powder, he recognized the need for dockage and moved to fill it. The location had the advantage of a new rock road recently completed south from (today's) Flagler Street. Lyon owned much riverfront property and had his home on old 14th Street (today's

S.W. 2nd Street). Some thought then that "... there will never be times, even during hurricanes, when the slightest danger will be experienced at this wharf from tide or other considerations." The following year, 1912, Charles F. Sulzner bought the 90 feet remaining between Lyon's wharf and the bridge. Sulzner first saw Miami "before the Railroad" while the Tequesta Indian mound was being removed. With encouragement from Flagler, he retired from his jewelry manufacturing business and returned to Miami in 1897. Here on the river, he filled an unsightly hole before building his own wharf. Thus a total of 290 feet of badly needed river dockage was provided. The hurricane of September 1926 brought a storm surge that raised the water level here about five to six feet, leaving many boats piled up below the bridge.

Figure 8B. Lyon Wharf, ca. 1912. (Historical Museum of Southern Florida)

Those docks were still there when Max Swartz established the East Coast Fisheries in 1933. Swartz got his start in 1918 by selling Maryland oysters in Florida to northern customers. This four-story structure is said to have been built in 1924. It was the second building to be built on an approach to a bridge. Originally Walter R. Miller's Riverside Fish Market, in the late 1920s it became Miller and Son Fish Market. Once used as a lobster canning factory, it became a fish market and restaurant. Fish were supplied to major cities across the United States and to Europe. In 1940, there was a hotel on the upper floors. Max's son David has run the business since the 1960s, with a large fleet of boats providing fresh fish directly to the plant. The restaurant expanded to two floors. Although lacking a good view of the river, East Coast Fisheries is a place with both character and quality where the customer can be part of the action and feel a little bit of old Miami by the river.

Figure 8C. East Coast Fisheries, ca. 1988. (Historical Museum of Southern Florida)

On the South Side of the River

On the south shore adjacent to S.W. 2nd Avenue—before there was today's bridge—B. J. Southall established the Biscayne Boats Works soon after the turn of the century. Better known as "Southall's," it included marine railways, repair shops and a boat storage basin. A long wharf ran along the shore connecting Southall's with the Jeffords-Way Machine Co. shop east of the line of S.W. 2nd Avenue. Southall's boat yard made the news in September 1915 when a fire destroyed the yard and 45 yachts belonging to wealthy visitors.

From 1918 into 1922, this was one of four Abijan Pelsang boat yards (see Chapters 6, 9, and 12). Among other things, Pelsang sold a unique "Disappearing Propeller Boat." With both engine and propeller mounted amid ship, the propeller could easily be retracted to give a perfectly smooth keel and very shallow draft. Many other advantages were cited. In 1921, J. Roy Tracy had a machine shop and a houseboat tucked in there by S.W. 2nd Avenue, while he lived nearby on S.W. 8th Street (see Chapter 17).

Pelsang sold in late 1922 to the Atlantic Construction Co., later the Atlantic Marine Boat Yard, which asked the city successfully for permission to close that (incomplete) portion of South River Drive between S.W. 5th Street and S.W. 2nd Avenue, because it was occasionally flooded in times of high water and Pelsang had marine railways extending across the street. The Brickell estate deeded a part of that strip to the city for the approach to the new bridge to be built there. The eastern portion of South River Drive was never completed there, and for a while S.W. 6th Street ran below the bridge.

The Atlantic Boat Yard (presumably the same company as Atlantic Marine Boat Yard) made the news in 1924 when the yacht *Cocoon* pulled in for repairs after being fired upon by the Coast Guard. This 50-foot yacht was a replica of one destroyed by fire at Elser's Pier the previous year, and had just been christened in a northern yard for M. M. Belding, a silk manufacturer from New York who was a member of the Miami Angler's Club and the Miami Boatman's Association. Two 150 horsepower Speedway engines gave her a speed of 32 knots. Spotted turning into Government Cut on her maiden voyage, the guardsmen first fired across her bow and then some bullets into the water which ricocheted into her hull, apparently expecting to find contraband liquor on board. They were disappointed as none was found. By the late 1930s, this location by the bridge served the boat yard of Jack Dunn Chris-Craft, Inc.

The Interstate-95 expressway crossed the river in 1968. The first fixed bridge on the mainstream of the river, it permanently blocked the passage of tall-masted ships that used to call at upstream boat yards. The land on the south shore below the Interstate-95 bridge plus some adjacent city property were used from June to October 1980 to help house the large number of Cuban refugees who fled Cuba that year from the port of Mariel. Miami's "tent city" became famous.

Figure 8D. "Tent City" beneath Interstate-95 expressway, 1980. (Historical Museum of Southern Florida)

That land known as "tent city," plus much additional city property upstream acquired during the 1970s, became the Jose Marti Park in 1984. This ground had been the site of a prehistoric Indian camp from about 400 A.D. Named to honor the famous Cuban patriot, Jose Marti Park provides a marine entrance to the area now known as East Little Havana. It is the most modern and best-equipped of the city parks on the Miami River.

❧

A canoe club for Miami was planned as early as 1916. Whether prospective members meant to canoe on the bay or the river is not known. By 1920, the Miami Canoe Club was established at 1305 South River Drive (today's 115 S.W. South River Drive). Here John D. and Agnes Dorn had their home and a boat livery. John Dorn was proprietor of the Canoe Club. That year the Miami Canoe Club had its own clubhouse, a two-story building with an open first floor porch facing the river. A 1921 newspaper photograph of the club members that year showed eight canoes tied side by side, with two or three people in each canoe, but the location is not evident. An archive photograph from the same period shows six canoes in the river with the clubhouse in the background. The rather formal dress of the people suggests that they had no fear of spilling into the polluted river. Indeed, among the activities of the club were "hurdling" their canoes, running one above another, and tilting, for which the members dressed in swim suits and surely expected to be dunked occasionally. Ted Hauser, Jeff Little and A. Collet were among early Miamians who enjoyed those sports. The free flow of fresh water from the Everglades that began in 1921 may have sufficiently relieved the pollution to permit such uses of the river for a few years.

In later years the club was also known as the Miami Kanoe Club and Miami Kanoe Klub. The Dorns were the "Pa" and "Ma" of the club. Pa Dorn built the clubhouse for the members and helped purchase canoes. The Dorns with Ted Hauser, Walter Coles, Lewys Greene, J. Hendricks and Lacy Vaughn were the founders. Twenty-five charter members attended the first meeting in November 1920. One member who was a musician, Harold Lamb, wrote a club song known as "Canoe Club Capers." Bay trips to places like Cape Florida, Fulford and Sunny Isles were common; as were races on the river, the bay and even the open Atlantic Ocean. A record was set when

Figure 8E. Miami Canoe Club clubhouse, ca. 1922. (Florida State Archives)

two members paddled from their clubhouse to Cape Florida and return in four hours and 13 minutes. Two other members paddled from Miami to Bangor, Maine. Six members went to Jacksonville for the first State Canoe Races. To help celebrate the opening of the Lawrence Park subdivision, the newspaper reported that members of the Miami Canoe Club competed with "Indians of the Seminole Tribe" on the newly completed Lawrence Park Canal (see Chapter 14). The Miami Canoe Club lasted through 1925, perhaps passing with the real estate boom or done in like so many other activities by the great hurricane of 1926.

(Mrs. Margaret Rogers Grutzbach, who came to Miami as a girl in 1906, remembers an earlier canoe club of which she was a member during about 1917 to 1920. Other members were Bob Jones and Frederick and Margorie Sulzner, children of the Charles F. Sulzners. That facility consisted of a tin building with a pool table and chairs and a boathouse, owned by Anton Hulman, who had the Calumet Baking Co. and was a winter visitor. It was located on the north shore of the river near today's Flagler Street. The club's commodore was Walter Godby; he and his wife had charge of the place. Four to five Old Town canoes were used. The club was for young people and much good, clean fun was enjoyed.)

By 1924, the much larger Dorn Hotel Apartments, a three-story building fronting right on South River Drive that was an irregular "U" shape with one wing extending to the river's edge, replaced the former clubhouse on that site. After World War II, it became the Riverview Hotel. With a ballroom and an unusually long bar, it was popular with local "river rats" and said to host such celebrities as the Dorsey brothers and Les Brown with their big bands, Jimmy Durante and Red Skelton. One old photo showed Bob Hope at the bar. By the 1970s, it had fallen on hard times and was a flop house. Robin and Claire Osterly bought the property from Thomas Stevens in 1978 and completely rebuilt the hotel with 110 rooms. Unfortunately, the Mariel "boat lift" of 1980 and the building of "tent city" just down the street changed the neighborhood drastically. In 1983 the building burned and was lost.

Across South River Drive from the former Miami Canoe Club and Dorn Hotel Apartments the Miami River Inn is now located, an elegant small hotel reminiscent of Miami's early days, yet near the heart of a vibrant modern city. Developed by Sallye Jude with an eye toward historic preservation, four former rooming houses built between 1906 and 1914 have been joined in a beautifully restored complex of 40 guest rooms, each with the ambience of early Miami but with all the modern conveniences. This property is on the National Register of Historic Places. The Inn is easily seen from the river and itself commands a nice view of the river and downtown Miami. Plans for the Miami River Inn include adding a restaurant in the old two-story building on the river immediately upstream from the former canoe club.

Adjacent to the Miami River Inn on the upstream side is the approach to the S.W. 1st Street bridge. Because those historic rooming houses in the old Riverside subdivision were built long before the bridge, today the restored Miami River Inn complex connects with the sidewalk of S.W. 1st Street by three walkways leading from the second floor level of each building. The owners of each of those three house lots deeded a strip of land to the city to permit construction of the bridge approach. The S.W. 1st Street bridge was the third of four bridges built under the same bond issue of 1926—bascule type, electrically powered, with four lanes. It was one of three similar bridges designed by Howard, Harrington and Ash, consulting engineers of Kansas City. The W. S. Lockman Construction Co. of West Palm Beach built the foundation and approaches. The Tampa Shipbuilding Co. built the spans. Street car tracks allowed for looping trolleys through the downtown section. Completed in June 1929, it still has the old silver paint, but will someday wear the green color of the Miami River Coordinating Committee's "rainbow plan." This bridge carries only eastbound vehicular traffic.

J. H. Tatum built the original Flagler Street (old Twelfth Street) bridge. Three brothers, Bethel Blanton, Johnson Reed, and Smiley M. Tatum, sons of a Georgia minister, came to Florida in the late 19th century, following different paths but joining together in Miami early in this century. They formed the Tatum Brothers Real Estate and Development Co., plus many other companies, and were instrumental in developing three Miami River subdivisions, plus other developments from Miami Beach to Florida City. Here on the west side of the river they developed their Riverside subdivision. To reach it they needed a bridge. The Tatums proposed building the bridge themselves. In September 1904, the county granted J. H. Tatum a permit to build the bridge. The city gave its approval to charge tolls in August. Final approval for its construction came later from the War Department (today we'd say Army Corps of Engineers). In addition to building a bridge, the Tatums paid to pave Flagler Street west to the Lawrence Road (today's N.W. 12th Avenue).

The Tatum bridge opened in early February 1905—just five months after local formal approval. It was a manually operated swing bridge similar to the one on Miami Avenue. The tolls were: 5 cents for a pedestrian, 15 cents for a one-horse carriage, and 25 cents for a two-horse carriage or automobile. (Twenty-five cents in 1905 was equivalent to about six of today's dollars!) The following year, Tatum offered his bridge to the city, which declined; so he offered free transit to all Riverside property owners. In 1909, the city assumed responsibility for the bridge and the tolls were eliminated.

A light trolley track across this swing bridge, built in late 1906, carried an electric trolley until February 1907. It failed in the financial panic of that year. In December 1915, service resumed on heavy 102 pound track, using battery-powered trolley cars. It continued through 1918, part of that time very cautiously across a temporary bridge. Then service ceased for a while, but resumed again in 1922.

An electric bascule bridge, again similar to the one on Miami Avenue, replaced the original swing bridge in just over a decade. M. F. Comer of Miami built it. The work began in mid 1916, and the bridge opened in November 1917. By the early 1920s, heavy vehicular traffic across the new bridge caused the city to propose a curfew between the hours of 6:30-8:00 a.m. and 5:00-6:30 p.m., during which times the bridge would not open. Comer's bridge served for almost half a century. Today's Flagler Street bridge opened in June 1967. It crosses the river a bit north of the site of the older bridges and carries mostly westbound traffic. This bridge wears the Miami River Coordinating Committee's "rainbow" color of green.

Chapter 9
Flagler Street to N.W. 5th Street (N.W. 7th Avenue)

Before the present Flagler Street bridge was built somewhat north of the old bridge, the Exotic Gardens had a store on the north side of the street by the bridge. That was south of today's bridge. The Exotic Gardens established their floral business in 1910. They built their store by the Flagler Street bridge soon after the bascule bridge of 1917 replaced the original swing bridge. It served there until well after World War II.

On the north shore just beyond where today's Flagler Street bridge crosses the river was a favorite place for the Indians to leave their dugout canoes when trading at Girtman's store, Brady's, or Burdines downtown. As many as 20 dugouts at a time landed there. From the turn of the century, Capt. Charles A. Mann lived in a large frame house at 1105 North River Drive (later 129 N.W. North River Drive) facing the river on the rise across the street, with a pier into the river below. He had many Indian friends and allowed the Indians to camp overnight on his property. On one occasion, a pregnant Indian woman who had just landed removed herself among some bushes to deliver her baby, then walked into town to do some shopping. Figure 9A shows some of Capt. Mann's Indian friends in front of his home. A photograph in *Miami 1909* by Peters shows Capt. Mann with the Tatum's Riverside subdivision across the river, still mostly pinewood. By the mid-1920s, his large home still stood almost alone on the rise with many private yachts docked on the river's edge, but his Indian friends continued to call occasionally.

Girtman's store was originally on today's East Flagler Street, but moved to N.W. 1st Street and Miami Avenue in about 1906. J. D. Girtman also had the confidence of the Indians and they enjoyed a mutually beneficial business: he buying their alligator hides, pelts, plumes and various foodstuffs, and they buying his ammunition, cloth, thread and other manufactured goods. His old frame store building was a landmark in early Miami until it was torn down in April 1912, about the time that the Miami Canal opened. Perhaps Girtman could see that draining the Everglades would take away the Indians' traditional means of making a living. He soon added to the size of his large grapefruit grove west of the city. But the Indians were not averse to shopping in the most modern emporiums. After trading at Girtman's, the Indians often went to Burdines. This Indian business accounted for a significant portion of Miami's merchandise.

A popular story was of an Indian named Tiger Charlie who visited Burdines shortly after they completed their five-story "skyscraper" in 1912 on Flagler Street just east of Miami Avenue. On that occasion Charlie bought all the bolts of a green calico material he liked. The purchase came to $108 (about $2,400 in 1990 dollars) and was the largest single sale since Burdines was founded 14 years before! Charlie paid in cash taken from an alligator "boodle" bag under his tunic.

Figure 9A. Capt. Mann's Indian friends, ca. 1902. (Thelma Peters)

Tom Newman built Captain Tom's Fish Market in 1932 close to where the Indians used to land. (Capt. Tom Newman was mentioned in Chapter 4.) Capt. Tom said: "This market was built for the benefit of the general public so they may buy fish at reasonable prices." In 1936, almost as an afterthought, he added the restaurant. He built an addition adjacent downstream plus a second floor to the original building where the restaurant faced the river. Capt. Tom's Fish and Oyster House was a popular seafood eating place for many years. He sold the building in about 1947, but it continued as a restaurant. It is said that the sale terms required retention of the name. Today, the building is occupied by Atco Marine Service, Inc., but on the wall facing North River Drive is prominently carved for all to see: "Capt. Toms says:—THIS MARKET WAS BUILT FOR THE BENEFIT OF THE GENERAL PUBLIC SO THEY MAY BUY FISH AT REASONABLE PRICES."

Lummus Park, so named in the mid-1920s after Commissioner J. E. Lummus, was Miami's first city park, begun in 1909. (Originally called "City Park," in the early 1920s it was sometimes called "Central Park.") Between N.W. 2nd and 3rd Streets, it extends from the river east to today's Interstate-95 expressway. Two of 38 lots were purchased from B. B. Tatum, the remaining lots from Flagler's Model Land Company. The Corps of Engineers determined where the seawall could be built, and an oolitic limestone ridge along the shore was removed to give a gradual slope to the river's edge where some 500 feet of mangrove were taken out. The city planned a grand promenade along the riverbank. Although nicely landscaped, this was a recreational park. A baseball diamond, tennis courts and greens for lawn bowling were provided, the latter sport continuing popular for at least two decades.

The author's great-grandfather, Richard Ashby, enjoyed bowling here through the 1920s, by which time the tennis courts were removed in favor of two additional bowling greens. In April 1925, *The Miami Herald* announced construction of "An attractive clubhouse ... in City Park for the benefit of the Miami Bowling-on-the-Green Club." By the mid-1930s, the seven-acre Lummus Park had 28 shuffle board courts, five roque courts, horse shoes, cards, checkers, chess, dominoes, croquet and bowling on the green. This was for the use of residents and winter visitors alike. Two bowling greens covered 24,000 square feet of perfect lawn, plus the clubhouse for bowlers. There were two sheltered and lighted pavilions for card playing, large locker rooms, eight player domino tables, etc. The park was active from morning into the evening. Lawn bowling was the elite sport. The clubhouse lasted into the 1970s.

Figure 9B. Bowling on the green at Lummus Park, looking east toward the clubhouse with the courthouse in the background, ca. 1927. (Romer Collection, Metro-Dade Public Library)

Also in 1925, the old Fort Dallas "long building" was taken down stone-by-stone and rebuilt here in Lummus Park by the Miami Woman's Club and the Daughters of the American Revolution (DAR). Begun by William English in the late 1840s and intended for slave quarters, it was completed by the Army in 1849 and used as troop quarters (see Chapter 5). After the Seminole

Wars, the building was used as a store, post office, as the county courthouse and as a residence. It was also a restaurant in 1925. In September 1929—well after its reconstruction in Lummus Park—the Miami City Commission granted the Everglades Chapter of the DAR use of old Fort Dallas as their headquarters or meeting place. In July 1933, the DAR installed iron grills for security over the doors and windows of old Fort Dallas. The following month, a newly installed clay tile roof collapsed, damaging the building when the supporting beams could not bear the heavier weight of the tiles that replaced shingles.

Near the old Fort Dallas "long building" is located the "Wagner House," moved here in 1981 from its original location near Wagner Creek and restored by the Dade Heritage Trust. Built by William Wagner about 1857 (see Chapter 10), it is the earliest preserved wooden house in Dade County. This and the long building are the two oldest buildings in Miami.

In 1949, the City of Miami leased the riverfront portion of Lummus Park to the Miami Pioneers, Inc. for $1 per year with the stipulation that this city property should be used "solely for the purpose of operating and maintaining a club house for the use of its members and for no other purpose." (This not-for-profit organization was incorporated in 1937.) The Pioneers built a clubhouse with funds from the sale of bonds, many of which were never redeemed because some members who purchased bonds chose that means of making a greater contribution. Some say that the clubhouse was designed by Miami's famous architect Walter C. DeGarmo. Although DeGarmo designed a clubhouse for the Pioneers, the present structure bears little resemblance to DeGarmo's architectural drawings. By the 1960s, the dock space and clubhouse were being rented commercially and the clubhouse was falling into disrepair. In the early 1980s, improvements to Lummus Park considered by the Parks Department included closing North River Drive so the upland park would connect with the river, removing the Pioneers' clubhouse building, constructing a new marina, restaurant, etc. They planned these improvements to benefit the public, especially the downtown business and professional communities, and to provide a more attractive river scene. Several years of negotiations proved fruitless and this property remains unsightly on the river, still unused by the public.

Adjacent to Lummus Park on the north is the Scottish Rite Masonic Temple. The Miami Scottish Rite was chartered in 1918. (The old Masonic Hall was on S.E. 1st Street near Miami Avenue.) Planning for a temple began that same year when the Masons purchased from Harry Tuttle a 75 by 240 foot parcel of land fronting the river in Fort Dallas Park, located directly in front of the old Fort Dallas buildings themselves (as reported by *The Miami Metropolis*). In 1921, the city traded the present Scottish Rite Temple site for property owned by the Masons (as reported in the *Metropolis*). Kiehnel and Elliott, an architectural firm of Pittsburgh and Miami, designed the temple building. It was said to include touches of Syrian, Greek and Egyptian architecture. John B. Orr, pioneer contractor and builder, constructed it without profit to himself (he being the illustrious potentate of the Mahi Shrine and builder of many other handsome structures in Miami). The Masons laid the cornerstone in December 1922, and completed the structure in early 1924. Rising three stories tall with four Doric columns on the street side, it is beautifully embellished and the ziggurat-shaped mass of the roof capped by a cupola are quite striking when viewed from the river. A large auditorium with 1,200 seats and a high ceiling has a stage and dressing rooms adequately equipped for operatic productions. Included also were a large ballroom, two lodge rooms and many lesser rooms. A modern ventilating system provided an exchange of fresh air in all parts of the building before the advent of air conditioning. It was meant to serve other Masonic groups of Miami as well. For many years it also served the public, with the large auditorium often made available for theatrical productions. The masons continue to use this beautiful building.

Figure 9C. Scottish Rite Masonic Temple, ca. 1930. (Matlack Collection, Historical Museum of Southern Florida)

On the South Side of the River

On the south shore by the Flagler Street bridge, the River View Apartments was in 1920 the first building erected on a bridge approach. Known also as the Galatis Building, this two-story structure had a third story added in 1921 to meet the demand for apartments with a view of the river. It had 26 apartments, each with private bath, and 159 feet of river frontage. Striped awnings covered all of the windows and thin square columns passed through a mansard roof. (This should not be confused with the Riverview Apartments located on S.W. 1st Street that had a view of the river, but were located on the far side of North River Drive.)

By 1923, the name changed to the Del Rio Apartments, with 22 apartments facing the river and full hotel services. Stores on the ground level faced Flagler Street and South River Drive. It also included a bar known as the Del Rio Grotto. Late that year, the Grotto was closed by circuit court

Figure 9D. Del Rio Apartments, ca. 1923. (Florida State Archives)

order for serving liquor, and declared a public nuisance, after Sheriff Allen and Solicitor Pine made three liquor raids on the place. In just over a week, the Florida Supreme Court lifted portions of that injunction for the soda fountain, confectionery and restaurant. It seemed a reasonable compromise for the time. In 1925, the Del Rio Apartments were sold by Galatis to H. L. Breslau, a prominent New York attorney.

Just above Flagler Street today is Natural Sponges, Arellano Brothers, Inc. Sponge fishing was once an important industry in Florida, but died in the 1930s due to disease that destroyed the sponges. A rebirth began in 1962 when the Arellano brothers established their business here on the river (see Figure 9E) It is one of those important industries introduced by recent Cuban immigrants. Sponges harvested in the Florida Keys and the Bahama Islands are purchased at the dock, then processed, packed, and shipped to northern markets, Europe and Japan. Many natural sponges piled next to the building may be seen easily from the river.

On the south shore near the bridge was one of the four Pelsang boat yards (see Chapters 6, 8, and 12). Much of the south shore in this section, and part of the north shore, developed with commercial fish houses and boat yards early in Miami's history. On the south shore opposite the Scottish Rite Temple was the Hollywood Boat and Transportation Co., owned by J. W. Young, the developer of the Hollywood-By-The-Sea subdivision. Here in 1924 they launched the *Jessie Fay*, a cruising houseboat for Young. One hundred and two feet long but drawing only three feet, she

Figure 9E. Modern day spongers at Natural Sponges, Arellano Brothers, Inc., ca. 1989. (Historical Museum of Southern Florida)

was the largest vessel built in Miami until that time. A crew of 10 served the owner and his guests in eight staterooms.

Fisheries had become an important industry by 1909, only 12 years after the city was incorporated. There were 14 major companies, employing 217 boats and 551 men. Although 1909 was thought to be an off year, two varieties, the Spanish and king mackerel, yielded 2,040,000 pounds caught and shipped from Miami. (Spanish mackerel then brought 8 cents per pound and king mackerel 5 cents per pound, equivalent to about $2.05 and $1.15 per pound, respectively, in 1990 dollars.) Catches were shipped north by both train and steamer or schooner. By 1973, there were 14 commercial fisheries on the river, or about the same number as six decades earlier. In 1990, the fishing industry netted an estimated 25 to 30 million dollars from the sale and distribution of stone crabs, lobster and mackerel. Clearly mackerel are still abundant, and there has been an increase in varieties traded with a tremendous increase in the value of the product. However, much of the catch today comes from foreign countries; and some of these fisheries, although located on the river, are not "water dependent"—they are really more for distribution and could be located elsewhere.

We have arrived at the Fifth Street bridge, crossing the river from where North River Drive, N.W. 7th Avenue and N.W. 5th Street meet on the north side—to where South River Drive, N.W. 8th Avenue and N.W. 4th Street join on the south side. This location was always the most narrow part of the river below where it forks. It marked the western limit of the original city of 1896, that limit being somewhat farther west on the south side of the river than north of it. Did Flagler's people plan someday to build a bridge here at the city's western limit? In January 1919, showing rare foresight, the City of Miami bought land at this location for a large sewer outlet and noted that this land "could be used as an approach for a bridge that might be built someday across the river at this point, which is one of the narrowest points, angling . . . ."

The day was not long in coming. The Fifth Street bridge opened in November 1925, being a double-leaf bascule type, electrically powered, with four lanes, 11 feet of vertical clearance and 77 feet of horizontal clearance. Built by the Comer-Ebsary Foundation Co., it remains today the only non-fixed bridge to "angle across" the river, all others crossing either north-south or east-west. This bridge was not yet a year old when the great hurricane of September 1926 struck Miami. The storm surge passed up the river to pile boats, houseboats and debris aplenty on the north shore below the bridge. At 67 years old in 1992, it is the third oldest bridge on the river system, and wears the Miami River Coordinating Committee's "rainbow" color of blue.

Figure 9F. Fish house on the Miami River, ca. l917. This scene is taken from today's Miami Avenue with the old Florida East Coast railroad swing bridge also visible in the center of the river. (Historical Museum of Southern Florida)

Chapter 10
Wagner Creek and the Seybold Canal

Wagner Creek was the main natural tributary of the Miami River, joining the river about one and a half miles from Biscayne Bay. It ran roughly north beside today's N.W. 7th Avenue to about 8th Street, then wound northwest on a course that passed through today's Civic Center and Comstock Park near N.W. 28th Street and 17th Avenue. Today, the creek has been channeled through the Civic Center and covered north of 20th Street to 17th Avenue, but the dry stream bed of Wagner Creek and some old cypress trees may still be seen running southeast to northwest through Comstock Park.

In the late 1840s, William English (see Chapter 5) built a coontie starch mill on Wagner Creek near the river. The manufacture of coontie (also spelled "comptie") starch from the tubers of the coontie plant (*Zamia pumila*), which grew profusely throughout the pine woods of the coastal ridge, was almost the only way for early settlers to earn cash money. It required laborious processing of the tubers and an abundance of fresh water. English's early mill was one of many built along the river in the 19th century.

William Wagner, born of German immigrant parents in 1825, was a veteran of the Mexican War who was wounded in 1847 and returned to Fort Moultrie, Georgia, to recuperate. There he married Eveline Aimar, a French Creole, probably on the federal military post. The laws of South Carolina then defined anyone with 1/32 black blood as a Negro and forbade interracial marriages. Eveline was about 15 years older than William and had been married. Perhaps it was their situation that inclined them toward a move to the Florida frontier.

Wagner's former Army unit was assigned from Fort Moultrie to Fort Dallas in 1855. Wagner joined with a Capt. Sinclair (or St. Clare), a sea captain with two schooners, and followed the Army to the Miami River to establish a sutler's store to serve the troops during the Third Seminole War (1955-58). Together with Capt. Sinclair, he built a steam-powered coontie mill on Wagner Creek. Perhaps it was on the site of English's earlier mill. In the late 1850s, he built a house about 50 yards back from the creek that would come to bear his name, located near today's N.W. 11th Street and 7th Avenue. It was a one and one-half story building of braced frame construction, with board and batten siding, and a gable roof with wooden shingles. It had a small porch with a shed roof. (This old house, moved and restored, was noted in Lummus Park.) Sinclair left in 1859.

In 1875, acting on a suggestion by the Right Reverend Bishop Rewot of St. Augustine who was visiting from Key West, Wagner built a small Catholic chapel, known as the "Little Church in the Pine Woods." Father Hugen of Key West dedicated it in 1876. This was the earliest house of worship in the Miami area since the Spanish missions. A Wagner granddaughter was married there that year, shortly after a hurricane in October that passed directly over Key West but somewhat west of Miami. The chapel burned in 1892.

The Wagners were friendly, outgoing people, helpful and well liked in the community. He managed to maintain good relations with both the Union forces and Confederate sympathizers during the Civil War. He was a true friend of and respected by the Indians. After living on the site for over a decade, Wagner filed for a homestead claim in 1869, and received a patent to 40 acres of land from President R. B. Hayes in 1877. He thought that was enough and did not request the full 160 acres allowed. Eveline died in 1888. Wagner managed to obtain a military pension that year, and his mill closed about the same time. He sold his property to Julia Tuttle in 1893, then bought it back from the probate court in 1899, and died on the land in 1901 at the age of 76. William Wagner was a true pioneer who lived to see the birth of modern Miami.

In 1901, a canal was dug from the head of Wagner Creek to drain the Allapattah Prairie. It was the first artificial tributary to be made on the Miami River system. For agriculture, this opened what came to be known as the richest farmland along the river. The Humbuggus Prairie up from the Little River and the Cutler Prairie were already famous for growing tomatoes and other vegetables.

In the late 1890s, "Alligator Joe" (nee Warren B. Frazee), opened an alligator farm and crude tourist attraction on the east side of Wagner Creek near its mouth. (He already had an alligator farm in West Palm Beach.) Joe was a large, fat man of some 270 pounds with a funny mustache but no chin whiskers. Loud and rough, he was the first person known to wrestle alligators for the entertainment of others. On his farm, just outside the city limits and seemingly "in the Everglades," he raised alligators and some crocodiles. Baby alligators he sold to tourists; the big ones he wrestled. His method was to wade into deep water to engage his quarry, going round and round with it while occasionally kicking up for air, then bringing the exhausted beast to shore where an assistant would help him secure its jaws with a rope. No doubt Joe's bulk was an asset. But the first person to do anything always makes it easier for those who follow! The tour boat *Sallie* made regular stops at Alligator Joe's place, while en route to Richardson's Grove and the rapids at the headwaters of the river.

For more than a decade, Joe took his show on the road to places like Coney Island, Boston, Kansas City and San Francisco, thrilling crowds everywhere. In late 1910, Joe returned home to trouble when he was ordered to vacate his land which was held under a lease. By April 1911, this property around the mouth of Wagner Creek was advertised for sale. Joe moved up the river to about 14th Avenue (see Chapter 12).

John Seybold was a German immigrant who came to Miami in 1896 to thrive as a baker and become a prominent citizen. Downtown he built the Seybold Building and Seybold Arcade on Flagler Street. In 1913, Seybold acquired the land where Alligator Joe's attraction had been near the mouth of Wagner Creek, plus much other additional land, and began to develop Spring Garden as an elegant subdivision close to the city with water access for yachtsmen. He built the Seybold Canal by straightening the lower portion of Wagner Creek, making it wider and deeper, and dredged a turning basin near 11th Street. By the spring of 1918,

Figure 10A. Alligator Joe beside one of his alligator pens, ca. 1910. (Historical Museum of Southern Florida)

Figure 10B. Alligator Joe's place on Wagner Creek, ca. 1903. (Historical Museum of Southern Florida)

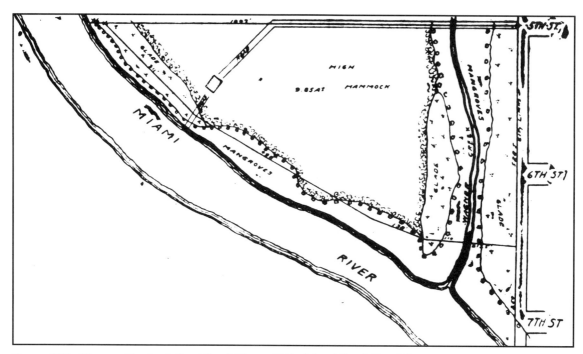

Figure 10C. Wagner Creek at the Miami River, 1911. (The Miami Herald)

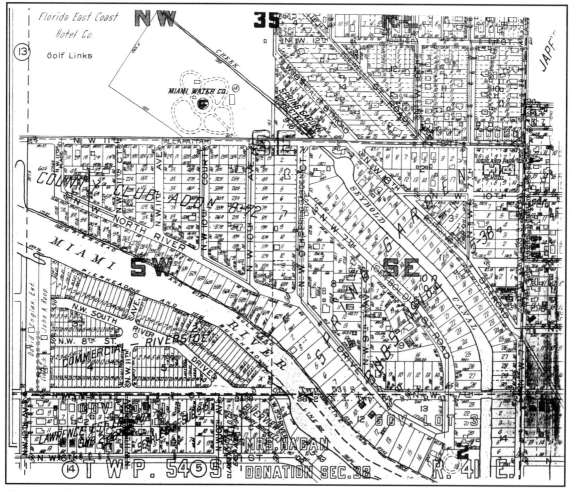

Figure 10D. Plat map of Spring Garden and Country Club addition, ca. 1918. (Historical Museum of Southern Florida)

it was essentially complete, with entrances from today's N.W. 11th Street on 9th Court and over the "humpback" bridge crossing his Seybold Canal on N.W. 7th Street. Today's N.W. 9th Court was Spring Garden Drive, and N.W. 7th Street Road was Seybold Drive. Seybold planned a permanent home for himself on the point where the Seybold Canal joins the Miami River. In 1917, he moved temporarily with his family into a large house that included his real estate sales office on the lot adjacent to the north which backed up to the canal. That building is gone while the large parcel of land intended for his permanent home remains vacant.

In January 1919, William Farnum came to town to star in the movie "The Lucky Charm," part of which was filmed in Spring Garden. The film's name was later changed to "The Jungle Trail." For a movie set, the producers built a "Hindu temple" on the Seybold Canal. Seybold liked the temple so much that he had a house of a somewhat similar appearance built on the north side of the turning basin at 11th Street. Actor Charles O. Richardson, son of Otis Richardson (see Chapter 18), lived in the house for many years. A granddaughter, Cyane Berning, was born in the house and lived there until 1990. That interesting old house with twin turrets received an historic designation in 1991 and will be renovated for an office. In recent years, several movies made in Miami have included Seybold's "humpback" bridge across the Seybold Canal.

Many of Miami's prominent citizens chose to make their homes in Spring Garden. These included Dr. Benjamin F. and Margaret Hodsdon and the Wanderell Camps, both on the river, Judge Frank B. Stoneman and his daughter Marjory in a house owned by *The Miami Herald*, Truly Nolen, T. D. Scherer, Redmund B. "Bunn" Gautier, W. C. Maynard, and Robin B. and Clara Mulloy whose son Gardner still lives there. Even so, the 1926 hurricane followed by the Great Depression

Figure 10E. "Hindu temple" building on the Seybold Canal, 1919. (Historical Museum of Southern Florida)

meant that fewer than half of the riverside lots were built on before the 1940s. Most homes in Spring Garden, including some on the Seybold Canal, have been well maintained or are being restored. Spring Garden retains a strong sense of community and remains a desirable residential neighborhood close by the Civic Center, the University of Miami-Jackson Memorial Hospital complex and downtown Miami.

Spring Garden was expanded a bit in 1923 to extend north of N.W. 11th Street to N.W. 8th Street Road.

A low bridge at 11th Street blocks further passage by boat.

Chapter 11
N.W. 5ᵗʰ Street to N.W. 12ᵗʰ Avenue

Two brothers, George and Samuel Wagner Freas, sailed from Philadelphia to Florida in 1902 in a 22-foot cat boat, eventually reaching Miami. As a result of that trip, their father, George Albert Freas, moved his family to Miami and built a large wooden gabled house in what today is Spring Garden. That house was near today's 9th Avenue on the north side of an unpaved road that became today's North River Drive. (The 1905 Official Map of the City of Miami and Vicinity shows a parcel of land belonging to Geo. C. Frier that extended from the Miami River north to today's N.W. 11th Street, approximately between N.W. 9th Avenue and 9th Court. Perhaps Geo. C. Frier sold to George A. Freas, or there were errors in the spelling of the name while recording that property.)

In about 1910, Samuel Wagner Freas with another brother, Warren, established the Miami Towing and Lighterage Co. in this location on today's North River Drive. Figure 10C, showing the mouth of Wagner Creek in 1911, includes a building at this very spot that was reached by a road running northeast a bit, then east to cross the creek on today's N.W. 7th Street. It seems probable that that was the Freas building. Their business lasted through the 1920s, but at a different location. The G. A. Freas home is not shown on that 1911 map, and may have been built later. Freas was a machinist in Pennsylvania, and opened a machine shop in Miami on today's N.W. 5th Street in about 1907. By 1916, he relocated the machine shop on the south side of the river. In the early 1920s, Freas joined with A. DesRocher to open a machine shop on the south side of the river near Miami Avenue (see Chapter 7). He appears to have retired in the late 1920s.

There were 10 children in that family, one of whom, Helen, taught at Riverside School and would row a boat across the river to school and back. At least one granddaughter, Margaret Freas, grew up in Spring Garden and was a close friend of Pat Mulloy. Margaret Freas Klein and Marcia Mulloy Petersen both fondly remember growing up in Spring Garden and what a wonderful place it was for children.

The north shore of the river today borders Spring Garden, treated in the last chapter in connection with the Seybold Canal. What is called Spring Garden has spread beyond its original bounds. Adjacent to the west is the Country Club Addition, with an entrance between square stone columns from N.W. 11th Street on 10th Avenue, but it is all generally considered to be Spring Garden. The M. F. Comer Bridge and Foundation Co. building remains on the river near 11th Avenue (see Chapter 16). Used by the company in the 1930s, in the 1980s it was a marine facility for the Miami-Dade Community College, but is now vacant.

An alteration of the area along the river began in the 1970s when a zoning change allowed condominium townhouses and apartments to replace private homes. This area is also a favored location for persons living aboard their houseboats or yachts. However, as mentioned previously, Spring Garden retains a strong sense of community and remains a desirable residential neighborhood with the Civic Center, the University of Miami-Jackson Memorial Hospital complex and Downtown Miami all within close proximity.

Back from the river near Wagner Creek was the Penniman Spring, a natural spring with considerable flow. (It was "Wagner's Spring" during the Third Seminole War.) Close by near N.W. 11th Street and 11th Avenue, Don Cosgrove dug a well about 60 feet deep to clear, pure water around the turn of the century. Cosgrove thought it reached a subterranean river. This was an early source of water for the City of Miami, the Miami Water Co. plant being built there and supplying a 30-inch main line.

Later, they drilled four additional wells 100-feet deep on the adjacent golf club grounds. By 1919, these wells began to turn salty from hard pumping and the city's well field had to be relocated farther inland. (In 1925, the city opened a new well on the municipal golf course which seemed to provide an abundant supply of fresh water, but the intrusion of salt water prevailed. Fresh water began to flow from the Hialeah well that same year.)

Noteworthy a bit farther north was "Halissee Hall" (meaning "New Moon" in Seminole), the beautiful three-story home of John Sewell—Flagler intimate, Miami pioneer merchant, county commissioner and Miami's third mayor. He was also instrumental in clearing the land and building the Royal Palm Hotel at the mouth of the river. Built of the native oolitic limestone beginning in 1912, Halissee Hall stood at the crest of a rise in a 14-acre estate with a grand entrance road to the southeast. Sewell said he chose that site because it enjoyed a better breeze than even along the river. Today, the house is preserved on the grounds of Jackson Memorial Hospital, north of the Florida 836 expressway. South of that expressway, two grand stone structures with tiled roofs and

Figure 11A. Old entrance to Hallissee Hall, the John Sewell estate, 1992. (Don Gaby)

bearing heraldic emblems—formerly marking the entrance to the grounds of Halissee Hall—remain where N.W. 11th Street Road (formerly Sewell Drive) joins 10th Avenue and 13th Street.

On the South Side of the River

The south shore developed slowly with several boat yards and fish houses by the 1920s. As the downtown building boom neared its peak in 1925, J. D. O'Brien paid $350,000 for 13 acres of land with 1,300 feet of riverfront on the south shore between 8th and 12th Avenues. (That was about half a million dollars per acre in today's money for largely undeveloped land.) He planned a grand apartment hotel of 1,000 apartments and 250 hotel rooms on this site. It was another dream that

Figure 11B. Former *Miami Daily News* printing plant, 1992. (Don Gaby)

went bust with the boom and the 1926 hurricane. That large parcel remained vacant into World War II. In 1957, *The Miami Daily News* built the large building still there today for their publishing plant. Later it was used by Metropolitan-Dade County for offices, and today it is used by the First Union National Bank for its operations.

The facility adjacent to 12th Avenue was formerly the U.S. Naval Reserve Armory, the center of much activity during World War II. It was used during the 1970s and 1980s by Metro-Dade County as a base for its marine patrol boats.

The western city limit of Miami was extended to 12th Avenue in 1911.

Construction of the 12th Avenue bridge began in 1927. It was the first of four similar bridges—electric power, bascule type, four lanes—built under the same Harbor Bond Issue of 1926. The E. F. Powers Construction Co. built it. A strike in Belgium ports, from where the steel came, delayed this project. The bridge opened to traffic in January 1929. This bridge makes a slight bend eastward while crossing the river and, until well after World War II, 12th Avenue became a dead end at N.W. 11th Street (North River Drive) which bordered the south end of the Miami Country Club golf course—today's Civic Center. It is painted the old silver color, but will be painted purple in due course under the Miami River Coordinating Committee's "rainbow plan."

Chapter 12
12th Avenue to 17th Avenue

There was an important natural feature along this stretch of the river. Between today's 14th and 16th Avenues the water was much less deep with large rocks in some places only a few feet below the surface. The river was also very broad here, but the current ran faster because of the shallow water and it seemed to boil across the rocks below. Mrs. Mary Hodsdon Shaw, whose family moved to Spring Garden in 1920, remembers swimming in that area as a girl and being able to stand on certain known rocks. Richard Ebsary, Sr. remembers that the tug boats of that period struggled against the faster current there.

Army Lt. I. M. Robertson wrote in the 1850s that one could take a boat of four-foot draft all the way to the headwaters of the north fork. Perhaps he found a channel through those "shallows." When the dredge *Miami,* drawing seven feet at the bow, moved upstream to begin excavation of the Miami Canal in early May 1909, she may have enlarged the natural channel a bit in order to pass through. Early tugboat captains followed a channel that was deeper and marked with sticks called the "twig channel." Those shallows appear to have been removed about 1921 in connection with the enlargement of the Miami Canal from its start at the Miami River to its junction with the South New River Canal. The engineers thought that enlargement of the canal would serve little purpose for drainage unless the river also was deepened where it was shallow or otherwise restricted a full flow of water.

In late 1910, "Alligator Joe" moved his alligator farm and tourist attraction from Wagner Creek (see Chapter 10) to the north shore of the river near 14th Avenue, today a county parking lot. Here he had a large place with a narrow gauge railway and one or more cars pulled by two mules, a mule on either side of the tracks, which led around the alligator pits for the benefit of tourists. Mrs. Margaret Rogers Grutzbach, who came to Miami as a girl in 1906, remembers Joe at this location and said he had one of the largest and heaviest alligators in captivity, about 18 feet long and grossly overfed, like Joe himself. Joe operated from this location only a few years before moving to Jacksonville. He continued taking his show on the road around the country until his death in 1915 at age 40 from double pleural pneumonia caught in San Francisco. The probate of his estate showed 148 alligators, 25 crocodiles, 500 baby alligators, plus various other animals. Within just a few years Henry Coppinger, Jr. would attain even greater fame as an alligator wrestler! (See Chapter 14.)

The great event of 1911 took place just across the Allapattah Road (later Allapattah Drive and today North River Drive) from Alligator Joe's place. Henry Flagler built a nine hole golf course north of today's North River Drive and west of today's 12th Avenue for the guests of his Royal Palm Hotel. As part of the City of Miami's 15th anniversary celebration, a Wright Brothers biplane was brought by train to Miami and assembled here for flight. In July 1911, aviator Howard Gill piloted the first airplane flight from Miami, taking off from the golf links. The amazed crowd, including many curious Indians, watched this strange machine circle the field. The following day, Gill climbed to almost 8,000 feet. Then he took E. G. Sewell, the celebration chairman, for a ride, making Sewell the first Miamian ever to fly!

Perhaps in part because the shallows near 14th to 16th Avenues marked the end of deep water navigation, or because the location was just outside the city limits, in 1913 Capt. George J. Pilkington began "the largest yacht basin in the south" on the site of today's Merrill-Stevens Dry Dock Co. above 12th Avenue. Here the water was said to be very fresh and free of the toredo worm that is a menace to wooden boats.

Pilkington was a boat builder from Tampa with 34 years of experience. He built three covered boat basins with eight feet of water throughout—78,000 square feet under cover with high hangar doors. There was also running water and electric lighting, fire protection and a large reading room and clubhouse for his guests. For the sake of the ladies, no alcoholic beverages were allowed, but ice cream was available. This large facility opened in early 1914. Regular car service was provided into town. By 1917, he built a new marine railway for hauling boats up to 450 tons, and the yard specialized in servicing electric boats.

With an eye to expanding his boat works, in late 1919 Pilkington bought an adjacent piece of property, the Ornamental Stone Works, that lay between his yard and today's 12th Avenue. Then he ran into trouble. During World War I he built a yard on Miami Beach in order to build barges for the government, but went bankrupt in that effort. By 1921, he seemed to be reestablishing himself in Fort Lauderdale.

Abijan Pelsang, who had three other boat yards on the Miami River (see Chapters 6, 8 and 9), bought Pilkington's large boat building, repairing and storage facility in 1921. Pelsang did not develop the additional property that Pilkington had acquired, but he did make some improvements including a deep west-east slip. In 1922, he hauled "the Lusitania of Houseboats," the *Nirodha*—125-foot long with 22-foot beam—the largest vessel hauled on the river until that time. By the end of 1922, Pelsang suffered an illness and sold the facility to a corporation formed by Roy C. Wright, Gus Miller, Sr., George W. Langford, and Gus Miller, Jr., businessmen of Miami and Jacksonville. (Langford's construction company built the McAllister Hotel downtown on Flagler Street and Biscayne Boulevard, plus several other important downtown structures. Gustav Miller was president and general manager of the McAllister Hotel.)

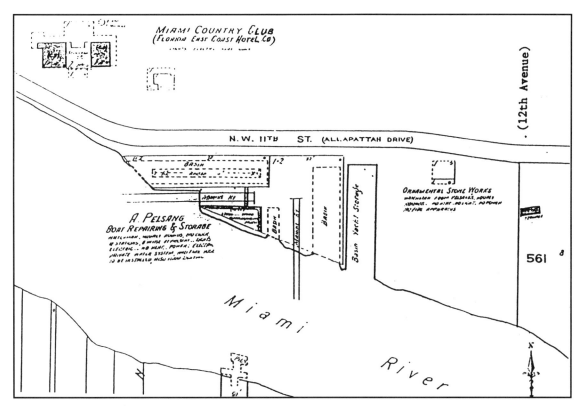

Figure 12A. Sanborn Insurance Co. map of Pelsang's Boat Yard, 1921. (P. K. Yonge Library, University of Florida)

Pelsang soon retired. He seemed to regain his health by April 1923 when he took the 45-foot cruiser *Eronel* out of storage for a fast run to New Jersey. By then this triangular piece of property had 900 feet of river frontage and was 400 feet long. The new company planned to continue operations under the Pelsang name. As superintendent they hired S. Thibault, formerly foreman at the Merrill-Stevens Co. of Jacksonville, Florida.

Perhaps because of this connection, the Merrill-Stevens Dry Dock & Repair Co. of Jacksonville purchased this fine facility in April 1923. (Merrill-Stevens was an old company, established in Jacksonville after the Civil War to manufacture steam boilers, later building riverboats in their entirety. During the Spanish-American War they did much business with Cuba and employed a tug boat captain, Napolean B. Broward, who later became governor of Florida and the man most responsible for draining the Everglades. In 1905-6 they built the hulls for two large Everglades dredges.) Merrill-Stevens soon added a new slip on the property adjacent to today's 12th Avenue formerly occupied by the Ornamental Stone Works. This expansion enabled them to service large dredges formerly sent to Jacksonville. They also serviced the finest yachts of that period. For example, they rebuilt James Deering's houseboat yacht *Nepenthe* by adding eight feet to the stern to eliminate its "chopped off" appearance and provide more deck space. All of the buildings were largely destroyed by the 1926 hurricane.

Merrill-Stevens rebuilt the modern yard that we know today, which by the 1930s was again serving such wealthy and famous yachtsmen as W. K. Vanderbilt and William Mellon. Alex M. Balfe was hired for a sales and managerial position around the mid-1930s. By then, Merrill-Stevens advertised "1,800 Ton Marine Railway for Dredge Work." Their main marine lift is now more than six decades old, but can smoothly raise 1,000 tons because of its unique design. Their wooden tugboat is more than 75 years old, having had several engine replacements, but is still the best for its job.

Figure 12B. Merrill-Stevens Dry Dock Co., looking across N.W. 12th Avenue, ca. 1985. (Alex M. Balfe, Merrill-Stevens Dry Dock Co.)

In 1938, Merrill-Stevens acquired the property across the river on the south shore (see below). The company also had a boat storage basin above 17th Avenue (see Chapter 14) and a full service marina in Coconut Grove.

Construction of the Interstate-95 expressway across the river downtown in the 1960s blocked the passage of tall-masted ships that formerly called at the yard, but Merrill-Stevens continues to prosper. It is the oldest boat yard on the Miami River and the longest under the control of the same family owners.

The Florida East Coast Hotel Co. announced construction of the "Miami Country Club" in June 1920, to be built near the river by the golf links and made open to the public. It was a beautiful Mediterranean style, two-story building with four corner towers, barrel tile roof and a huge screened porch, located inside the bend in today's North River Drive immediately west of Merrill-Stevens. It opened with a grand party in January 1921. This building lasted into the 1970s. Today the Civic Center occupies the former site of the clubhouse and golf links.

Figure 12C. The Miami Country Club as seen from across the river, ca. 1921. (Florida State Archives)

The area on the north shore west of the golf links developed as a fine residential section. During the late 1910s, the St. John's Park subdivision began next to the river and the Ocoee Park subdivision began back from the river and west of the golf links. Many people built nice homes here. The finest was that of S. Bobo Dean, editor and later owner of *The Miami Metropolis*, Miami's first newspaper, from 1905 until 1923. Dean first lived downtown on today's Biscayne Boulevard, then on the "southside" of the river, before moving to the north side in 1922. He built a beautiful three-story house on a 175 by 400 foot riverfront lot on the west side of 15th Avenue. It had the high ceilings and spacious windows that kept Miami houses cool in summer before the advent of air conditioning. The ample grounds were famous for their lush landscaping. (See Figure 12D.)

The Mahi Shrine acquired the S. Bobo Dean house and demolished it for a parking lot in 1989. The site may be recognized by the large cannon formerly in the riverside yard and today still aimed across the river toward Grove Park. This cannon is one of several from the *H.M.S. Winchester*, a fourth-rate British warship of 60 guns that was lost off Elliot Key in a hurricane in September 1695. The cannons were found and salvaged by Charles Brookfield, Hugh Matheson and others in 1938 and 1939. (Other *Winchester* cannons are up the river at Hardie's Yacht Basin, at the Historical Museum, the Biscayne Bay Yacht Club and the University of Miami.)

Figure 12D. S. Bobo Dean's house on the Miami River, ca. 1925. (Matlack Collection, Historical Museum of Southern Florida)

Upstream from St. John's Park, adjacent to today's 17th Avenue, was the Miami Gun Club—"on the river near the golf links"—as early as 1904. It had a 420-foot dock for yachts. During the 1920s, this area was also being developed for residential and business use. Today, the York Rite Masonic Temple and two three-story apartment buildings occupy the site.

On the South Side of the River

In 1850, George Ferguson, having lost his land and mill at the headwaters of the north fork (see Chapter 18), moved downstream to a parcel of 40 acres on both sides of the river above today's 12th Avenue. He probably chose the site because of the high ground on the south shore with a beautiful view down the river, and because it was at the end of deep water navigation in the river. Near the end of today's N.W. 13th Court, he built a large two-story house, the lower floor serving for a store and post office, a wharf and beautifully developed grounds.

Ferguson added an ingenious horse-powered mill—the horse riding a treadmill to drive the machinery rather than circling a vertical drive shaft as at other horse- or mule-powered mills. He used it for making his "Arrowroot" coontie starch, and for grinding corn and other grains. Ferguson had a contract to produce high quality coontie starch for an English firm, but a long dry spell allowed the river to turn brackish and ruined the business of quality starch making which required an abundance of fresh water.

George Ferguson became the post master when the government established a post office (in his home) in 1856, although the mail boat from Key West came only once a month. He later sold his place to George Lewis, a blockage runner during the Civil War, who was taken prisoner by Capt. English in 1861. It was the Lewis place that Capt. English burned in part to convince Dr. Fletcher to swear allegiance to the federal government as told in Chapter 5. In 1906, the ruins of a former home, perhaps Ferguson's, were found on this site in the modern Rivermont subdivision near 13th Avenue. These ruins included a great chimney, a deep well and stone terraces leading down to the river.

In 1897, General Samuel C. Lawrence bought a large tract of land including the south shore of the river from 14th Avenue to about 19th Avenue, south to S.W. 8th Street, east to 12th Avenue, and west below the south fork. Lawrence was a Union Army general during the Civil War. He was a wealthy New Englander who thought Miami had the ideal climate and used to spend his winters here, usually at the Royal Palm Hotel.

On his 700 acres he developed a large grove, a dairy, and a garden where he loved to receive visitors. He spared no expense to have the best grove and dairy, with the most modern equipment, and the Lawrence estate soon became famous. By 1907, he had steam powered irrigation with 12,000 feet of pipe and two 6,500 gallon tanks. Water was drawn from a spring-fed well 12 feet in diameter and 10 feet deep, and when drawing water at 100 gallons per minute the water level was reduced only three-eighths of an inch! Today's 12th Avenue was known as Lawrence Drive. Gen. Lawrence died in September 1911. His caretaker's house on 12th Avenue near S.W. 6th Street stood until November 1920. The guest house in his garden (today part of Sewell Park) lasted into the 1960s (see Chapter 14).

The Tatum Bros. Real Estate and Development Co. acquired the old Lawrence estate in 1912. They soon began to fill in parts of the shoreline on the river. They subdivided the land into small parcels to sell. However, development of this south shore did not begin in earnest until the 1920s.

Fordham's subdivision was platted just above 12th Avenue in 1921. In about 1924, the Waldeck-Deal Dredging Co. moved to this site from Cook's old dock (see Chapter 6). George A. Waldeck was president, Oriel Blunt was vice president, and B. A. Deal was secretary-treasurer. Their dredges *Deal* and *Marion* filled many of the artificial islands in north Biscayne Bay. In May 1925, the *Marion* began building "the largest dry dock in the south." A neighborhood delegation petitioned the City Commission to stop Waldeck-Deal from building the dry dock because it was a "public nuisance," had lowered residential property values, and because the company had torn up a recently laid sewer line. They claimed that residential land values there would soon exceed the property's commercial value. Waldeck-Deal kept their office and dock at this location, but by August completed their dry dock and yard at a different location on the river. Perhaps they moved from this site later that year because the neighbors were a nuisance, or maybe because their business decreased after the peak of the real estate boom of the "Roaring 1920s." In any event, that property still had commercial value. For over half a century until 1990, it was well known as the Howard Backus Towing Co.

The Backus family came to Miami from Connecticut via Colorado and Washington, D.C., where Howard Backus was born. They arrived in Miami in 1903. F. W. Backus and his wife Annie made the news in 1916 by driving their Ford car off the open draw of the old Avenue D (today Miami Avenue) bridge and into the river. The bridge arm was up and there was no light to indicate that the bridge was swung open. Fortunately, they landed on an old scow in shallow water and were not injured.

Howard Backus married Daisy in 1923 and son Fred was born during the great hurricane of 1926. F. W. Backus and a partner, Charles Tremblay, bought the property on the south shore by 12th Avenue in late 1925. They completed dredging boat slips where Waldeck-Deal began a large excavation for their dry dock. Soon they deeded 10 feet of their property for construction of the 12th Avenue bridge. Here they had a machine shop and served as distributor for Mianus marine diesel engines. During the Great Depression, they bought a tug boat named *Atlas*, the first of three by that name, when the Atlas Rock Co. went bankrupt. They had the contract to haul sand for building the Overseas Highway to Key West in the late 1930s, then for the Rickenbacker Causeway. After Tremblay ran into financial trouble, Backus bore the costs for the property, and Howard Backus bought out the Tremblay heirs in 1940. Commercial activity on the Miami Canal above

Figure 12E. Former Howard Backus Towing Co. tugboat *Atlas* wearing the colors of Florida Marine Towing Co., 1992. (Don Gaby)

27th Avenue picked up during World War II and Backus participated in that effort. After the war, the Antillean Marine Shipping Corp. became their customer.

The Howard Backus Towing Co. was a partnership between father and son until 1961, after which it was incorporated. By the 1970s, Backus and Hempstead (see Chapter 16) were the two principal towing companies on the Miami River and Canal, with grandson Fred Backus running their operation and that company towing the larger ships. Their fleet of two large tugs, the *Atlas*, and *Anita Backus*, and three smaller tugs, was ideal for towing the size of ships that can transit the Miami River and Canal. In 1990, Backus sold his five tug boats to Florida Marine Towing Co., that company using the Backus boat basin as a base of operations. The *Anita Backus*, wearing the Florida Marine Towing Co. colors, is now the *Banjo*.

Adjacent to the west was Debagory's boat yard and dry dock. Merrill-Stevens acquired their boat basin in 1938. They used it in a limited way until 1986, then greatly improved that property with large new hangars and slips to 200 feet. During 1991, a large portion of the high rock ridge was cut away to provide space for dry storage and boat service to the west. Looking up the adjacent avenue from the river is a good way to view the depth and character of the oolitic limestone ridge that runs along this stretch of the river's south shore.

Adjacent to the west was Debagory's boat yard and dry dock. Merrill-Stevens acquired their boat basin in 1938. They used it in a limited way until 1986, then greatly improved that property with large new hangars and slips to 200 feet. During 1991, a large portion of the high rock ridge was cut away to provide space for dry storage and boat service to the west. Looking up the adjacent avenue from the river is a good way to view the depth and character of the oolitic limestone ridge that runs along this stretch of the river's south shore.

The Rivermont, Oak Terrace and Grove Park subdivisions along the south shore of the river developed during the early 1920s. They represented the finest residential property along the river, being situated along the high ridge in that area. Many large oaks remain from the original tropical hardwood hammock that surmounted the ridge, together with a variety of well established citrus trees from the old Lawrence Grove.

Oak Terrace, together with adjacent parts of Rivermont and Grove Park, was transformed during the 1960s and 1970s into today's City of Miami senior citizens housing center. Three residential towers are prominent from the river. The western tower of 13 floors is called the Robert King High Tower, named in honor of Miami's beloved, five-term mayor of that name. Superbly designed for the local climate, all apartments run entirely across the width of the building with a double set of floor-to-ceiling jalousie windows that permit full control of breeze, light and privacy without the need for air conditioning. The central and eastern towers of 13 and 12 floors, respectively, built much later, are called the Haley Sofge Towers, named in honor of Haley Sofge, 13-year director of Miami's "Little HUD" (Metro-Dade Housing and Urban Development Department). Sofge came to Miami in 1957 as an expert on housing for the elderly and pioneered several innovative programs that were adopted nationwide. He integrated public housing in Dade County before President Kennedy's executive order made it mandatory. Here he was responsible, among other things, for these three tall residence buildings. Besides the nicely landscaped riverside grounds, on the street side of the complex one may find the "Haley Sofge Oak," a large old oak tree saved from the bulldozers by redesign of a building.

Grove Park was an especially desirable residential area, situated on the high ridge overlooking the country club and golf grounds across the river. Work began in 1916 toward "leveling" the riverfront by filling. B. B. Tatum announced development of this subdivision in September 1920. He advertised it as "The Million Dollar Sub-Division." Indeed, plans called for a riverside park, a centrally located neighborhood park, its own water works, gas connections, street lighting and ornamental entrances. Strict building restrictions ensured a high quality residential area. Regular street car service on N.W. 7th Street was anticipated. At the time it was just outside the city limits, yet very convenient to downtown. Ten residences were built by 1923, while others were under construction. Oddly enough, the larger waterfront lots were slow to be built upon.

In 1924, there were two riverfront homes. The first is the beautiful old two-story house on the ridge appearing behind the Florida-836 expressway support columns as seen from the river—said to be built in 1923 by Roddey Burdine, but occupied later by his brother John. (Roddey preferred to live on Miami Beach.) The second, just upstream, was the home of B. B. Tatum, the developer of Grove Park. He moved from downtown in late 1924 to a two-story home at the foot of 15th Avenue. It can be seen from the river across from the large parking lot next to the Mahi Temple Shrine. From the river it appears to be three stories with a red tile roof. It could easily have a basement. A broad staircase leads up from a double row of royal palms in the riverside yard (some now dead and never replaced) to a porch once graced with an ornamental stone balustrade.

A third early home may also be seen from the river, that of "old" Judge Tom Ferguson built in 1937, at the northeast corner of South River Drive and Park Lane (16th Avenue), a divided drive to the river's edge. Less easily seen from the river, it appears behind large trees approximately across the river from Bobo Dean's old *Winchester* cannon on the north shore. Two slender columns rising two stories stand by the entrance on Park Lane.

Figure 12F. Entrance to Grove Park, ca. 1922. (Historical Museum of Southern Florida)

There were only four riverfront homes in Grove Park by 1938, all east of Park Lane. Houses on the riverfront west of Park Lane were not built until after World War II. All of that property is said to have been the "Vogel estate," the owner of which wanted to build a garage-apartment there. When the neighbors objected to a change of zoning, he built the high wall around the property with only the single wooden door opening onto Park Lane near the river. When houses were built later, individuals made necessary breaks in that wall. That property is recognized from the river today by the high wall and the row of tall royal palms along the river's edge.

Some of Miami's most prominent families chose to live in Grove Park. Besides the Burdines, Tatums, and Fergusons already noted, worth mention were the Fred M. Bottshers, George E. McCaskills and Senator F. M. Hudson, all on the south side of South River Drive. Mrs. Margaret H. Bohnert and Matthew J. Bohnert had riverfront homes. Unfortunately, their homes facing the river and Senator Hudson's home, plus others, were taken for construction of the Florida-836 expressway in the 1960s. The Grove Park subdivision included a row of residential lots along the west side of N.W. 17th Avenue, some also taken for that expressway; plus several deep riverfront lots that were taken for the Lawrence Park Canal in the early 1920s and for today's 17th Avenue bridge approach in the late 1920s. In recent decades, much of the waterfront of Grove Park has become a favorite place for persons living aboard their boats or houseboats. Even so, Grove Park, like Spring Garden, retains a strong sense of community.

The 17th Avenue bridge was the fourth completed and farthest upstream of several bridges funded by the same bond issue of February 1926. It is one of three similar bridges designed by architects Howard, Harrington, and Ash of Kansas City—electric power, bascule type, with four lanes. The W. S. Lockman Construction Co. of West Palm Beach built the foundation and approaches. The Central Station Equipment Co. of Miami built the spans. It opened in July 1929. Circular islands formed part of the approach on each side of the river, "as an aid in the direction of traffic." Although more than a decade older than the 27th Avenue bascule bridge currently being replaced, and surely with more frequent openings, this bridge appears to have had better maintenance and still serves well. Its color is red under the Miami River Coordinating Committee's "rainbow plan."

Note: Of the five new bridges across the Miami River approved by the Harbor Bond Issue of February 1926, only four were completed. Voting citizens approved all five of those bridges by large majorities. A proposed bridge near N.W. 2nd Street—some suggested a joint span for N.W. 2nd and 3rd Streets—was approved by a vote of 853 to 71, but was never built. It surely would have taken a significant portion from the waterfront part of Lummus Park. We are fortunate it was never constructed.

Chapter 13
Lawrence Park Canal or "Caves Canal"

Running south from the Miami River immediately west of 17th Avenue is the Lawrence Park Canal, known by "river rats" as the "Caves Canal." W. A. Williams cut this beautiful artificial waterway through the high oolitic limestone ridge along the south side of the river during development of his Lawrence Park subdivision in 1921-22. E. G. Sewell Memorial Park borders the stream here where many subtropical trees grow along the high banks and join their branches overhead. Two turns close together bring one to a low bridge at South River Drive (N.W. 11th Street). Just south of the bridge on the west side are the caves.

These caves began as natural solution holes in the tropical hammock that once surmounted the ridge. As part of the General Samuel Lawrence estate from 1897 until his death in 1911, and then until 1921, these solution holes or "tunnels" were never mentioned.

W. A. Williams began development of his Lawrence Park subdivision in November 1921. The centerpiece was to be a grand inland waterway. Williams knew of these solution holes in the ridge and had his engineer follow that route in excavating the waterway to take advantage of the easier digging.

In February 1922, Eddie Polo starred in the movie "Robinson Crusoe," filmed here to take advantage of this uncommon terrain. In the film, Polo spent one night in an oak tree, and made his home in a "tunnel," probably a solution hole that opened onto the low ground on the south side of the high ridge. In a later report, the dredgeman described how the western rock side of the canal collapsed into a large solution hole during the excavation. Soon the developer began boasting of both tunnels and "caves," and by 1923 they had become the "Seminole Caves."

Historian Dr. Thelma Peters, nee Peterson, came with her Miami High School senior class in April 1922 for an evening picnic in Lawrence Park by the caves. She had not known about them before that visit, and must have been among the very first Miamians to view these caves. Williams appears to have enlarged the natural solution holes or tunnels to make much larger caves into which people could walk. Later owners have further enlarged the caves in various ways.

Today there are two large caves. One has an entrance onto the waterway with another entrance onto the low ground on the south side. A second cave has two entrances onto the low ground and another entrance on the north side where a stairway carved into the rock leads to the top of the ridge. These caves are mostly manmade.

For a while there was easy public access and many Miamians remember playing in these caves. John "Bud" White, Miami High School class of 1939, well remembers being initiated into his high school fraternity in 1938. The ceremony took place in the eastern-most cave and ended with him being pushed into the waterway. Other friends of the author played in the caves during the 1940s and 50s.

Figure 13A. Eastern cave of the Lawrence Park Canal, 1991. Another entrance faces directly on the waterway to the right. (Don Gaby)

Figure 13B. Western cave near the Lawrence Park Canal, 1991. A rear entrance stairway leads up to the ridge beyond the concrete floor slab above the cave. (Don Gaby)

On early plat maps this area of the caves is shown as "Pirate's Cove." It was a popular name given to at least two other places on the Miami River (see Chapters 14 and 16).

Former county commissioner Arthur Patton, Jr. purchased this property along the south side of South River Drive and bordering the Lawrence Park Canal in the 1970s. He built a home of unique design on the ridge partly above the caves. While Patton lived there, an Indian woman came to his door asking to see the caves because, she said, she was born in one of them. Perhaps her mother had come from Coppinger's place nearby, also known as "Pirate's Cove." One of these caves would have been a protected and private place to give birth, especially during the winter tourist season when a cold northwest wind might blow. (See next chapter.)

This land and Patton's house became the property of the Miccosukee Indian Tribe of Florida in the early 1980s. (The U.S. Secretary of the Interior approved the Miccosukee constitution in 1962.) Here, they opened a Miccosukee embassy in November 1984. This act caused a stir among Miami's consular corps. Since other countries have their embassies and ambassadors at Washington, a Miccosukee ambassador in Miami would outrank the local consuls. A protest was made to the U.S. State Department, some discussion followed, with a compromise solution that seemed pleasing to all parties. The Miccosukees agreed to call their facility a "cultural embassy." Although their cultural embassy contained few Miccosukee artifacts, it did contain many flags of foreign countries that had been visited. It all burned down early one morning in 1988. Only the raised concrete slab floor of Patton's former home remains on the ridge above the caves.

The low ground beside the caves was originally a "Japanese" garden built by Gen. Lawrence. In the waterway along this stretch, Williams planned a "sunken garden," a true subterranean garden on the floor of the waterway. Also planned was a series of metal arches to cross the waterway and be lighted at night. The main entrance to Lawrence Park was from N.W. 7th Street by the turning basin. When Williams died prematurely in March 1923, much of his dream died with him. One wonders what might have resulted here had Williams lived.

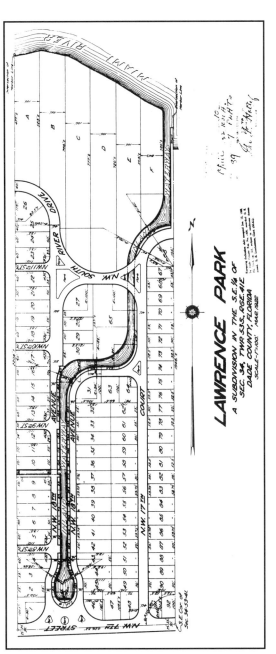

Figure 13C. Plat map of Lawrence Park subdivision, 1922, with its centerpiece inland waterway carved out by W. A. Williams. Although the writing is sideways and upsidedown, north is to the top. (Public records of Dade County)

Proceeding along the waterway, one passes through some of the original residential area of the Lawrence Park subdivision. (Part of the waterway was moved north when the Florida-836 expressway was built.) The waterway reaches a turning basin by N.W. 7th Street within sight of the Orange Bowl. It was built 30 feet wide overall, wider at turns, and the turning basin was 80 by 100 feet. Here one large metal arch was completed to span the basin and the lights were turned on in January 1923, making a beautiful reflection down the waterway. In February 1923, the newspaper reported a "Gala Sports Night" on the new waterway where a team of the "Seminole tribe" competed with a team from the "Miami Canoe Club" (see Chapter 8). (The Indians customarily poled, rather than paddled, their dugout canoes.) There was a stone "tori" entrance by 7th Street which lasted until recently. When it opened, advertisements for Lawrence Park several times claimed that the triple-screw yacht *Grayling III* brought many visitors and prospective customers to the turning basin. They said the *Grayling III* was 93 feet long, but one Miamian remembers it as about 65 feet, a size more able to easily have proceeded to the turning basin.

In recent decades, this beautiful artificial waterway has been neglected—allowed to fill with sediment, debris and fallen branches. It may be difficult for any but the smallest boats to pass through to the Florida-836 expressway bridge. In 1991-92, the city rebuilt the turning basin and that portion of the Lawrence Park Canal south of the Florida-836 expressway with new seawalls, storm sewers designed to contain most pollutant runoff, some landscaping and improved adjacent streets.

Chapter 14
17th Avenue to the Fork (19th Avenue)

All of the land in this section including the river and north to the line of today's N.W. 14th Street was originally part of the quarter-section of land deeded to George Marshall by President Zachary Taylor in 1849. Most of the north shore below the fork was little used until the late 1930s, except by Indians who often camped there. Part of the north shoreline was a sawgrass mud flat, while in other spots it was made up of mangroves, bays and oaks. After the Army Corps of Engineers deepened and widened the river in the early 1930s, it consisted almost entirely of dredged fill and remained undeveloped.

The Merrill-Stevens Dry Dock Co. (see Chapter 12) bought the property on the north shore adjacent to 17th Avenue in 1939. They built a yacht storage basin there in 1940 under a Reconstruction Finance Corp. loan. It consisted of three deep slips covered by a large, trapezoid-shaped metal hangar, designed to make optimum use of the space available. It could take boats up to 180 feet but with limited vertical clearance. Later they added a longer slip with a marine lift adjacent to the west. These were used into the 1970s. (See Figure 14A.)

In the early 1980s, the old Merrill-Stevens yacht storage basin and the large vacant property adjacent to the west were acquired for construction of the River Run Condominium. This 10-story condominium apartment building was originally meant to be built in three phases or units, but only the first unit was completed as planned. Where units two and three would have been constructed, a different builder added the six-story River Run Apartments in the mid-1980s. This complex of rental apartments became the Miami River Yacht Club in the late 1980s. The condominium and rental apartment complex share some facilities such as the marina and swimming pool.

Adjacent to the west is Kadey-Krogen Yachts, Inc., easily recognized by the Miccosukee Indian chickee built near the river's edge. This property was originally part of the Marshall land grant of 1849. Laura Hill Weatherington, a widow, and Elmer J. Lehman owned it in the 1930s. They sold to Mildred (Mrs. Hugh) Martin's mother in 1937. Her property came to include a small frame house with Bermuda roof that Hugh Martin moved up the river on a barge in the late 1950s (see Chapter 19). Florida Marine Construction, a marine salvage company, rented the property for their operation until 1985.

Figure 14A. Merrill-Stevens 17th Avenue yacht storage basin, hangar, and boats, ca. 1941. (Romer Collection, Miami-Dade Public Library)

James S. Krogen, yacht designers, began in 1960 with a location on the Miami River in Grove Park. Neighbor problems caused them to relocate nearby on N.W. 7th Street. Kadey-Krogen Yachts was formed in 1978 to import yachts designed by Krogen but built in Taiwan. Art Kadey was murdered in the early 1980s, and their business partner, Buz Labbee, bought Kadey's interest while the firm retained the old name. In 1985, they purchased the property adjacent to the Miami River Yacht Club and moved to their present location near the fork of the river. Their office had been a model apartment for the nearby River Run Condominium while that was being built. They added the Miccosukee Indian chickee by the riverside in 1986.

On the South Side of the River

As mentioned in Chapter 12, Gen. Samuel C. Lawrence, a wealthy New Englander who spent his winters at the Royal Palm Hotel, purchased much of the land along the south shore of the river in 1897. To the east of today's 17th Avenue he developed a grove and dairy that became famous. Here west of 17th Avenue to about 18th Place and south to N.W. 7th Street, he built a beautiful garden where he loved to receive visitors. He made a great effort to collect exotic tropical plants, laid out bridle paths for the convenience of his guests (some of which were later paved for automobiles), built a guest house and made a concrete boat slip and boathouse. The entrance was from N.W. 7th Street. The "Lawrence estate" was a renowned and favorite place for celebrated people and others to visit. Gen. Lawrence's guest house—the ruins of which can still be seen in today's E. G. Sewell Memorial Park—was a two-story structure with twin columns at the south-

Figure 14B. General Lawrence's former guest house, 1922. (*The Miami Herald*, Miami-Dade Public Library)

Figure 14C. The ruins of Gen. Lawrence's former guest house, 1991. (Don Gaby)

side front entrance. Steps at the northeast corner lead from the porch to a famous "avenue of royal palms" that ran down to the river's edge. Gen. Lawrence loved to serve his special blend of tropical punch, made from the fruit of his own trees, to the many people who came to visit. A guest book, sadly lost, contained numerous names of world famous visitors.

Although half of the original palms from that famous "avenue of royal palms" were dead after almost a century, that avenue of palms could still be recognized easily by the two tallest royal palms in the park at the upland end of the "avenue" and two clumps of royal palms where parent trees once stood and dropped their fruit—until the passage of Hurricane Andrew in August 1992. Many palms and trees fell to the southwest from northeast winds in the initial onslaught, but the taller of those two venerable royal palms held until forced to succumb by the stronger east winds, falling due west. The water level rose to about five and one-half feet during Andrew's passage, flooding the lower portion of the park along the river.

After Lawrence's death in 1911, Felder Lang (see below) acquired the west portion of the Lawrence estate. He already had Incachee Grove on the west. In 1913, Howard Humphries acquired all of this property. In those years it was still a favorite stop for the "rubber neck wagon"—so named because the passengers were constantly stretching their necks this way and that in order not to miss any of the scenes to be viewed from the bus. Other tourists came to the old Lawrence dock by tour boat. A number of motion picture films were made there, including *The Lotus Flower* starring John Barrymore during 1918-1920 when the parents of Celia Mangels, Miami pioneers, occupied Gen. Lawrence's former guest house. In 1921, W. A. Williams bought that property. (See Chapter 13 on the development of the Lawrence Park subdivision and canal by Williams.)

In early 1921, W. A. Williams and his wife Hoda H. had a home in Royal Poinciana Park, a subdivision that he developed adjacent to the west of Lawrence Park. After purchasing the Lawrence Park property, they moved into Gen. Lawrence's former guest house. By then it had been improved to make it more comfortable as a home. Williams died prematurely in March 1923 at the age of 41, after an illness of three weeks. He was a well known real estate broker, one of the oldest members of the Miami Anglers Club, and active in many civic affairs.

Williams' widow, Hoda H., married William M. Hope about 1926. She continued to live in Gen. Lawrence's former guest house with her new husband, at the modern address of 1801 N.W. South River Drive. The house was neither large nor elegant, but it was two stories with a porch surrounding the front and river sides. The kitchen was separate from the house. It lasted into the 1960s. As mentioned above, two columns and part of the main entrance on the south side, plus the stone steps from the porch on the river side, still remain in Sewell Park. Gen. Lawrence's old boat slip and boathouse, constructed in the first decade of the l900s, lasted into the 1950s. His concrete boat slip remains in Sewell Park, but is now neglected and badly silted.

In 1964, the City of Miami acquired the former William H. Hope estate of about 10 acres for a city park. The Parks Department demolished Gen. Lawrence's former guest house in 1969. An inventory of the native and exotic plants made at that time included a very long list of species. After some development, it was dedicated as the E. G. Sewell Memorial Park in honor of Miami's famous pioneer, early mayor and lifelong promoter of the "Magic City." The unique combination of native and exotic flora, and its beautiful site on the Miami River, make this one of the outstanding parks in Dade County. Although many trees and palms blew down in Hurricane Andrew 1992, so many remain that this park will soon be almost as beautiful as ever.

Figure 14D. Modern view of E. G. Sewell Park, formerly the Lawrence estate garden, 1991. (Don Gaby)

Adjacent to Sewell Park is the former Edenholme subdivision, originally part of the old Lawrence estate, today the site of the Harbor View Hospital at 1861 N.W. South River Drive. Near the turn of the century, this property belonged to H. Price Williams, overseer of the Lawrence place next door. He had a two-story bungalow, a boathouse, citrus grove and barn. Felder Lang purchased it in December 1904 or soon after. Lang was from Georgia, fought in the Civil War, and came out of the war as a second lieutenant in command of a cavalry company. He served two terms in the Georgia legislature before coming to Florida. Lang and his wife Martha named the place "Incachee," like their home by the sea in Georgia where they lived when first married. The Incachee Grove became famous, a frequent stop for the tour boat *Sallie* bringing tourists from the Royal Palm Hotel, many of whom had never seen a citrus grove. Felder Lang soon became active in the Miami community. In 1911, Lang appears to have acquired the adjacent portion of today's Sewell Park to the east, later the Royal Poinciana Park subdivision developed by W. A. Williams. In November 1913 as he began to suffer blindness, Lang sold his beloved Incachee Grove and moved to a new home downtown.

Howard Humphries acquired the property and held it in the late 1910s. By the early 1920s, this was the estate of H. E. R. Rogers. In 1942, Dr. P. L. Dodge founded the Dodge Medical Center here. Dr. Dodge kept his yacht in Gen. Lawrence's former boathouse (today in Sewell Park) into the 1950s. In front of today's hospital is a magnificent old silk cotton tree (Ceiba pentandra) probably planted by General Lawrence about the turn of the century and nurtured by Felder Lang. It was a large tree when Rogers lived there. Today it has buttress roots taller than a man. This huge, beautiful tree, now about 90 years old, is probably the oldest and perhaps the largest exotic tree in

Miami. Broken some by Hurricane Andrew, it stands today as tall as ever. Although the top of this tree is visible from the river at a distance, it well deserves a visit by land also.

Figure 14E. Patrick Calnan, the author's grandson, in front of the silk cotton tree of the old Lawrence estate, today in front of Harbor View Hospital, 1861 N.W. South River Drive, 1990. (Don Gaby)

Coppinger's Tropical Garden, Indian Village and Alligator Farm was west of Harbor View Hospital, where today there is the River Club townhouse complex. Together with the adjacent empty lot it was noted as Wilson's farm in the 1870s, and Indians camped there during the late 19th and early 20th centuries. Henry Coppinger, Sr. was born in Cork, Ireland, where his father managed the estate of Lord Middleton, considered one of the most beautiful holdings of that country's nobility. He emigrated to America at the age of 19 and lived in Washington, D.C., before moving to Orlando, Florida. There he lived 15 years before moving to Miami by wagon in 1898. Coppinger laid out the grounds of Flagler's Royal Palm Hotel and his Colonial Hotel at Nassau in the Bahamas, helped Gen. Lawrence with his estate, and planted an avocado grove on the old Charles Deering estate. In 1911, he bought 10 acres of land (running south to N.W. 7th St.) and settled here near the fork of the Miami River.

Coppinger's Tropical Garden opened in 1914 and soon attracted thousands of visitors. It contained many rare plants including the brick red bougainvillea which he introduced.

In 1917, recognizing the plight of the Indians as a result of draining the Everglades which eliminated their traditional means of livelihood, Coppinger invited several Indian families to set up a small village where tourists could view their way of life, crafts, etc., and the Indians could earn a living while adapting to white ways. Coppinger's Tropical Garden and Indian Village came to include seven "chickee" houses, five permanently occupied during the winter tourist season, plus a detached chickee for medical care. By 1922, it included a crafts shop. This attraction was one of those places also known as "Pirate's Cove." The tour boat *Dixie* made two scheduled 45-minute stops daily. Although described by some as "demeaning," the Indians worked voluntarily and were well paid and cared for.

Important note: Wherever "Indians" are mentioned on the Miami River in the 20th century, they probably were of the Miccosukee tribe, not of the Seminole tribe, although in years past most people and the newspapers were not aware of the distinction.

Figure 14F. Henry Coppinger, Jr., the "Alligator Boy," capturing a five-foot 'gator in the Everglades, ca. 1920 (*Miami Tribune*, Historical Association of Southern Florida)

Coppinger's is best remembered for the alligator wrestling of Henry Coppinger, Jr. Born in 1898, young Henry would have been about 15 years old when "Alligator Joe" (see Chapters 10 & 12) left Miami. He probably watched Joe and learned from that, but he developed his own technique. Unlike Joe, Henry was a small man but very strong. As a boy he would go into the Everglades to capture baby alligators, later capturing mature alligators with his bare hands. Thus he gained experience in the wild. He would wrestle any alligator up to nine feet long by diving into deep water, subduing the reptile with his bare hands, throwing it up onto a raft or canoe, then putting it into a semi-comatose state by stroking its stomach—a method he discovered for calming the beast.

By the 1920s, Coppinger was taking a large collection of alligators on tour around the United States, once was severely bitten on the arm in Kansas City.

By then the attraction was known as Coppinger's Tropical Garden, Indian Village and Alligator Farm. A popular act he performed at the large swimming pool of the Royal Palm Hotel was done with the assistance of an Indian. A large alligator would be placed in the pool. Henry and the Indian would board a dugout canoe, with the Indian poling it to the alligator's location. Then

Figure 14G. Coppinger's Tropical Garden, Indian Village and Alligator Farm, ca. l925. (Don Gaby, from a slide of unknown origin)

Henry would dive off to capture his prey, subdue it, and land it in the dugout or on a raft. Later he performed much the same act in the new Venetian Pool in Coral Gables, but from a modern canoe and without the Indian helper. He gained national fame for his skill and courage during the 1920s and 1930s. Although the Miccosukee Indians learned to wrestle alligators from Henry, they never performed at Coppinger's, but later at Musa Isle and elsewhere.

Coppinger's Tropical Garden, Indian Village and Alligator Farm began to decline in popularity during World War II. Construction of the Florida-836 expressway during the 1960s, which isolated the attraction, was its death knell. Nothing remains but the original Coppinger house, built in the early l910s (seen above in Figure 14G). Originally located at 1901 N.W. South River Drive, this interesting, two-story, clapboard house of pecky cypress was moved south a block or so to 1110 N.W. l9th Avenue in 1984. The original house never had a raised first floor, and the Indians were said to sleep inside in bad weather. Like so many older homes, this house survived Hurricane Andrew with only the loss of a few asphalt shingles and a bent TV antenna—in part because of its "Bermuda" style or "hip" roof (sloping toward all sides) that is so very well suited to the hurricane belt. Today the River Club townhouse complex occupies the former site of Coppinger's Tropical Garden, Indian Village, and Alligator Farm.

During the Second Seminole War (1835-1842), there was an Indian ambush of two boats with soldiers returning from "Fort Miami" (a temporary fort more like a camp site) up the river under the command of Capt. Samuel L. Russell. It resulted in the only recorded fatality due to military

Figure 14H. Tour boat *Dixie* at Coppinger's landing, ca. 1925. (Historical Museum of Southern Florida)

combat on the Miami River during the long period of the Seminole Wars (1835 to 1858). Military historians mention the incident on the river and give the date, but without location or details. A letter reprinted in Nile's National Register, Washington City, March 1839, the post return from Fort Dallas, March 1839 and a later account from an early Miami newspaper allow one to reconstruct the scene and action. The author believes that the ambush occurred here, just below where the north and south forks of the river join. A more advantageous location would be difficult to find. Here, near today's Harbor View Hospital, is a crest of the ridge with 15 feet elevation that would have commanded a fine view up both the north and south forks of the river while the tropical hammock concealed the Indians. At the fork, the confluence of the two streams would increase the speed of the current just as the river makes two bends, occupying the soldiers with their boats.

The ambush occurred on 28 February 1839. From their vantage point on the ridge, the Indians fired on the two boats. The first round of rifle fire passed entirely over the heads of the soldiers, confirming that the Indians were firing from high ground or "an eminence." The soldiers immediately made for the opposite shore. As Capt. Russell's boat landed, he stepped ashore and, turning to rally his troops, was struck by three enemy bullets and killed instantly. Second Lt. Charles E. Woodruff, in the second boat well upstream, rushed to assume command and gather his men. The account states that "the action continued for more than an hour when they retreated." Had the soldiers landed on the south shore, a bayonet charge or other close fighting would not have lasted so long. But they landed on the north shore near today's Miami River Yacht Club and River Run Condominium complex, and merely exchanged fire across the river. Unable to recover their boats under the guns of the Indians who were well concealed, the soldiers probably withdrew and marched the three miles by land to Fort Dallas.

We have arrived at the "fork" of the Miami River. We are about three miles from Biscayne Bay and only one mile from the original eastern edge of the Everglades. In the 19th century, and probably for centuries before that, persons entering the Everglades from the Miami River—Indians, settlers, soldiers or visitors—customarily did so via the south fork to our left, because it had less current and a much lower rapids at its head. Returning from the 'Glades, they would use the north fork, where they could shoot the rapids or go around them to find a swift current for going home. The much larger north fork was always considered the main stream of the river. The south fork was just as long but only about one-third as broad, and it was really more of a tributary.

Chapter 15
South Fork to Salinity Dam (28ᵗʰ Avenue)

In this chapter we take a side trip up the south fork of the Miami River. The large parcel of land ahead of us at the fork itself, bounded on two sides by the north and south forks of the river and by the Everglades to the west, was often called an "island" in the 19th and even into the 20th century. It must often have appeared so before drainage of the Everglades, especially during the wet season when the Everglades stretched to the western horizon like an inland sea of water and grass, with an occasional hammock island to break the monotony.

The south fork was called "Marshall's Creek" through the 1860s and the land between the forks was called "Marshall's Island" after an early settler, George Marshall, who lived on the river as early as 1828 and came to stay in August 1842 at the end of the Second Seminole War. Marshall obtained a quarter-section of land (160 acres) where he had settled—from the U.S.A. by President Zachary Taylor in 1849. It was conveyed under "An Act to provide for the armed occupation and settlement of the unsettled part of the Peninsula of East Florida." This was an act of the congress to encourage settlement at the end of the Second Seminole War. Marshall had his home on the north shore in today's Durham Park. It had a very fine spring of water. His large garden and fruit grove were well known attractions. On the south shore he had a large field of bananas.

Marshall was prone to drink—indeed, to drunken binges—perhaps as an antidote to the hordes of mosquitoes and horseflies. In early 1861, probably in such an inebriated condition, he shot and killed the 10-year-old son of William Wagner at George Lewis's place (Ferguson's old place down the river). While the local people sent for the sheriff, Marshall slipped away and was never seen again. In February 1861, in a Warranty Deed not acknowledged by George Marshall, his land was conveyed to Robert R. Fletcher. (Dr. Fletcher was mentioned earlier downriver in Chapter 5.) Here on the south fork he had a coontie mill across from what had been Marshall's house. Fletcher's mill was about where Allied Marine is today at 2051 N.W. 11th St. During the 1870s, Fletcher's land was owned by a farmer named Wilson and the south fork then was known as "Wilson's Creek." How it came to be called the "south fork" is a mystery.

On the north shore, and extending across to the north fork, F. H. Rand of the Miami Real Estate Co. platted a subdivision in 1919. Some filling of the east point was done using material from the widening of S.W. 1st Street from the river to 22nd Avenue, and streets were laid, after which a new plan developed—then all was laid to rest by the 1926 hurricane. The Army Corps of Engineers added additional fill on the east point and along both shores of this subdivision while deepening and widening the river in the early 1930s. In the late 1930s, James Durham Hobbs and associates developed today's Durham Park with 99 homesites. About 18 houses were constructed before World War II.

The beautiful two-story house on the north shore adjacent to 22nd Avenue was built by Dr. Albert L. Neuenschwander, who had Miami's first optometrist's shop. He brought his family to

Miami in 1914, and built the house in 1924. The riverside garden once was used for a movie set. Across the stream on the south shore next to 22nd Avenue, his son Lawrence established the South Fork Marine Service, a small boat yard typical of many along the river in those early years. It operated under that name from 1942 until 1958. C & F Marine, Inc. occupies the site today. Another son, Roy, lived nearby on the north shore of the south fork until very recently. Other family members continue to occupy the old Neuenschwander house.

Figure 15A. South Fork Marine Service, ca. 1950. (Roy Neuenschwander)

On the South Side of the River

The favorite place to swim in the Miami River in the 1920s was on the south fork below the 22nd Avenue bridge, about in front of today's Allied Marine. There was a 10-foot-deep hole, perhaps marking the mouth of a former spring, with a sandy beach on the south shore, and only a gentle current.

The Maule Ojus Rock Co., with its plant in Ojus, Florida, changed its name to Maule Industries and purchased the site of today's Allied Marine on the south shore in the mid-1920s. It moved its operations there in about 1936, and remained until the end of World War II, by which time it had several other yards in the Miami area. During the mid-1940s, Allied Marine acquired that property. As this is written, Allied Marine is for sale as that company consolidates its service operations up the Atlantic coast.

(C & F Marine on the south shore by the bridge was mentioned above in connection with Neuenschwander.)

The original fixed wooden bridge across the south fork of the river on 22nd Avenue was built in 1908, together with a similar bridge across the north fork on 27th Avenue, making them the only bridges above Flagler Street. J. C. Baile, an early grower and later businessman, promoted these bridges and solicited funds from individuals for their construction. They provided Miamians for the first time the opportunity to drive almost entirely around the upper river—"to circle the 'Glades"—starting from Flagler Street on the south and connecting with the Allapattah Road (later Allapattah Drive and today North River Drive) on the north side. A more substantial bridge replaced the original wooden bridge in 1916. Today's bridge is the third, completed in 1965.

West of 22nd Avenue

The south fork of the river was always smaller, less well known, and less popular. It may also have been more beautiful, with a more winding course, and narrow enough that trees could cross it in places. Raccoons and opossums were hunted and trapped by a few people in this area into the 1920s. Montgomery Ward and Sears & Roebuck were ready buyers for the hides and furs. Just west of 22nd Avenue the stream broadened, with a bend toward the north which was deep and called the "Alligator Hole." The "old sentinel" cypress tree in the parking lot of today's Polish

Figure 15B. Indians on the south fork of the Miami River, ca. 1904. (Florida State Archives)

American Club grew near this deep hole, now filled. Farther along near 24th Avenue was a small island created in the mid-1920s and known as "Fern Isle." It was made by digging a deeper channel around the south side of a boggy area with small cypress. Now long gone, the city's "Fern Isle Nursery" on the nearby north shore retained the name for a while.

Between the Alligator Hole and Fern Isle, Gus Mitchell built an elegant private home in the early 1920s. The entrance was from N.W. 14th Street, but the spacious grounds ran south to the south fork of the river. Mitchell built his house of the native rock, and it featured a large indoor swimming pool that connected with the living room, all set in beautifully landscaped grounds. He thought that area would be chosen for similar nice homes.

In November 1924, Harry L. Katz, described as a "prominent hotel and restaurant magnate of Atlantic City," bought the place. Katz was reported as paying $65,000 (well over a million dollars in today's money) for this property in a sparsely populated area beyond the city limits. He intended to convert the house into a modern restaurant and cabaret to accommodate 300 people. The changes were described as frame construction with a high dome for special lighting effects. (Perhaps he covered or filled the swimming pool.) The new "Silver Slipper" cabaret opened on New Year's Eve of 1924, featuring Vincent Lopez and his dance orchestra. Professional dancers featured included Eddie Cox and Loretta McDermott, world champion whirlwind dancers Layman and King, oriental dancer Thelma Edwards and Minnie Allen, "Atlantic City's favorite." The Silver Slipper closed that first season in late March. It continued as one of Miami's favorite night spots, at least through the 1930s.

Don Lanning, a professional entertainer who married actress Roberta Sherwood, ran the Silver Slipper during the '30s. He continued to book many well known acts and performers. Afterward for many years, the property was not used. For a while, Don Dickerman was the proprietor and it was called "Don Dickerman's Pirates' Den." Today, the Police Benevolent Association (PBA) occupies the site, with a more modern building for their clubhouse.

It is fascinating and perhaps significant that on the very day in November 1924 that *The Miami Herald* reported Katz's purchase of the Mitchell home, the *Miami Tribune* reported one Harry I. [sic] Katz mysteriously murdered in Los Angeles. There Katz was described as "the lone love wolf of Los Angeles gold coast," reputed "former violinist to the czar of Russia," also as a master musician, yachtsman, and art collector, not to mention notorious lover. His funeral was attended by his father who was a peddler of kitchen utensils. One wonders if this was this the same or a related Harry Katz?

On the South Side of the River

There is little development along this stretch of the south fork. Prior to World War I, the Heights of Riverside subdivison developed on the south shore with a broad avenue leading from today's N.W. 7th Street to the water. All property owners enjoyed riparian rights. Today it is mostly Fern Isle Park and city park maintenance property.

Just beyond the fixed 27th Avenue bridge is a salinity dam installed in about 1970. The rapids of the south fork of the river were located a short distance on the other side, at the eastern edge of the Everglades. Some old cypress trees on the south shore still survive from before Everglades drainage. Two German immigrant brothers, John and Nicolas Adams, built a home nearby on the last dry land in the mid-19th century. It was a spacious house with a large rock chimney, a garden, and a hand-operated coontie mill. One of the brothers was assistant lighthouse keeper at Cape Florida, and maintained the barracks at Fort Dallas between the wars. They built "Adam's Landing," a boat landing on the south shore by the rapids, in the early 1850s. It was the point from which military parties entered the Everglades during the Third Seminole War. Here the rapids were only a foot or less, and with much less current than on the north fork. (Military parties also entered the Everglades from this point during the Second Seminole War, before the Adams brothers arrived.)

Figure 15C is copied from a sketch map in the Cartographic Branch of the National Archives. It depicts part of "the route taken by the expedition under Capt. S. K. Dawson, 1st Art, which left Fort Dallas March 1st 1855 and after penetrating the Everglades in canoes returned March 7th—had reached a point forty-three miles distant from Ft. Dallas, measured along the route." It also shows Adam's Landing at the edge of the Everglades.

As early as 1903, most natural streams along the lower east coast of Florida were being dug out or extended. By then there was already a plan to "take hold of" the south fork of the river by blasting out the rapids and running a ditch westward four to five miles. That effort was delayed until August 1908, when Comfort and Huyler hired J. R. Tatum to direct the drainage operations. The Tatum dredge moved up to the south fork in late 1908 or very early 1909. (Note that this private project proceeded the start of the Miami Canal by several months. This proximity of dates may explain why some older Miamians confuse the "dynamiting" of the rapids of the south fork with those of the north fork—which were never removed.)

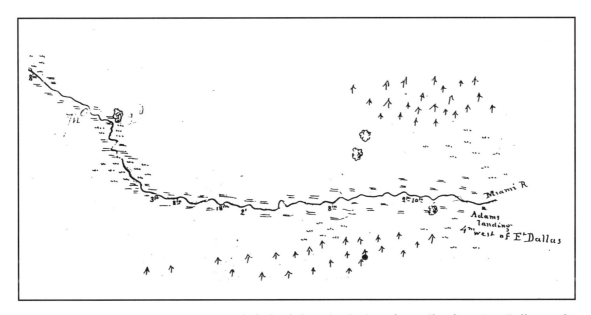

Figure 15C. Adams's Landing on the south fork of the Miami River, four miles from Fort Dallas, at the edge of the Everglades, 1855. (U. S. National Archives)

W. R. Comfort was president of the Reid Ice Cream Co. of New York, which consolidated with the Borden Milk Co., of which he was a major shareholder. Comfort also had an interest in some 20 other firms. John C. Huyler had a candy manufacturing business in New York City. Together they formed the Seminole Fruit & Land Co., and planned an experiment to drain a small portion of the Everglades for the cultivation of sugar cane in order to produce their own sugar. They had an option on 35,000 acres of Everglades land west of the head-waters of the south and north forks of the river. While dredging the Huyler-Comfort Canal, also known as the Seminole Fruit & Land Co. Canal, Tatum also dredged out some of the south fork itself. By March 1909, before the Miami Canal excavation began, Comfort and Huyler had dug almost a mile of their canal. About a third of the "falls" or rapids was removed, with a wooden dam built to retain water for the dredge.

By 1910, they planted some 300 acres with cane brought from Cuba and were planning a large sugar processing plant. That October, Huyler died in New York at 64, but his heirs pledged to continue his effort. Huyler's participation was soon forgotten. For whatever reason, the project slowed, and not until 1917 was the canal finished. By then it could connect with the Tamiami Canal. (For a few years, that portion of today's Tamiami Canal that joins the Miami Canal was called the "Comfort" or the "Cross-cut" Canal.) In 1918, Comfort built himself a home in Miramar and became one of Miami's prominent citizens. He moved to the Patricia Hotel in later years. In 1928, Comfort died in New York at 70 years of age.

For a few years after 1908 there was a "South Fork Tour." Capt. Ed. F. Youngs took his little launch *Ava* from the Royal Palm Dock, up the south fork of the river, "climbing the rapids, and on into the Huyler-Comfort Drainage Canal." The wooden dam, where a portion of the south fork rapids were blasted out in 1908, remained into the 1920s. It was easy to drive over the remaining rapids with a small power boat. Among the trees found along the south fork were live oak, bald cypress, bays, willows, custard or pond apple, and ficus—plus palmettos and reeds. It must have been a wild and delightful trip.

The natural course of the south fork was altered slightly in the 1960s for the Florida 836 expressway and its exits to 27th Avenue. Although 27th Avenue is being improved as this is written, most of the old cypress tress along the south fork in that vicinity survive. Navigation is blocked by the low fixed bridge and salinty dam.

Chapter 16
North Fork (Mainstream) to 22ⁿᵈ Avenue

On the north shore, just above the fork itself, was a cove that extended north and then west, at least by 1917. Whether it was originally a natural cove is not known. By the 1920s, this feature was known as "Pirate's Cove"—a third place on the river to bear this name. Eastward from this cove to beyond the fork, the land was originally saw grass mud flats. In 1921, Capt. Hicks Allen, in partnership with Roy C. Tracy, established Allen's West End Boat Yard on the north shore at the fork. At the time it was farther upriver than any other yard, but in spite of the distance it soon prospered. Later this yard was known as Tracy's West End Boat Yard, perhaps because Tracy bought out his partner, or simply because he ran the yard and it became associated with his name.

In any event, it was an unusual yard in that Allen and Tracy cut a channel for boat storage from the Miami River just below the fork to the east end of the cove above the fork. They covered this with a metal hangar 60 feet wide by 325 feet long. Thus a narrow island was created along the north shore of the river at the fork. In addition, they cut another deep slip on the east side directly north from the river, covered by a smaller hangar at its terminus. Tracy's West End Boat Yard originally had two marine railways with a third added later. Boats up to 100 feet could be hauled. The yard lasted into the late 1930s and is still remembered by some rivermen. Tracy himself went into the funeral business.

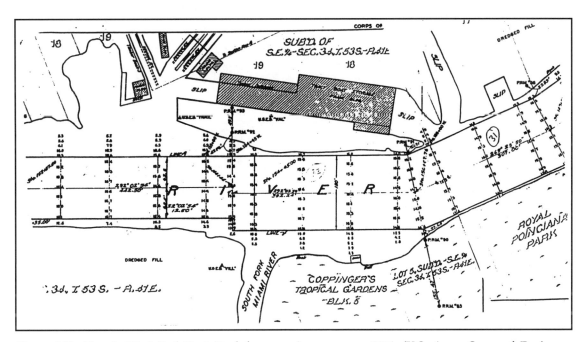

Figure 16A. Tracy's West End Boat Yard from an Army survey, 1934. (U.S. Army Corps of Engineers, Jacksonville District)

In 1939, Louis Nuta, Sr. purchased Tracy's Yard plus additional property. Nuta dredged out much of what had been land, including the narrow island, to build the large boat basin that we know today. The following year he built the large building with a curved roof that is there today.

During World War II, most of the newly developed property was taken over by the U.S. Army as a repair base for a large number of air-sea rescue boats used for the Miami International Air Depot (MIAD), today part of Miami International Airport. The Army constructed many smaller buildings for barracks, a mess hall, repair shops, supplies, etc. About a hundred men were stationed there, plus some German prisoners-of-war. Two dozen or more boats could be kept at the yard. Nuta retained control of the deep slip and some land at the end of his yard, where he converted pleasure boats for use as a patrol service in southeast Florida waters—mounting depth charge racks and painting the boats dark gray for nocturnal duty. During those war years it was difficult to obtain help with many men drafted or otherwise in the military services. Nuta therefore began to hire Indians from across the river at Coppinger's Tropical Garden and Indian Village. These Indians would swim to work, holding their clothes above the water with one hand, then dressing on the north shore. They would return home at the end of the work day in the same manner.

Louis Nuta, Sr. was an outstanding mechanic who came to Miami in 1925 and established an automobile repair business on N.W. 36th Street. He was also an aviator and hard hat diver, and for a hobby sought treasure from sunken ships on the Florida reef. In about 1930, he founded the Marine Motors & Parts Co., located downtown on the north shore of the river just below the 5th Street bridge (today upstream from Joe's Seafood Restaurant). His home and workshop were across North River Drive on a lot that ran through to N.W. 5th Street.

Figure 16B. Nuta's Boat Yard, looking north with the river in the foreground, ca. 1943. (Louis Nuta, Jr.)

During the Prohibition Era (1920-33), Lou Nuta, Sr. became famous for his ability to tune Army surplus Liberty aircraft engines adapted for marine use from 400 horsepower to as much as 450-470 horsepower. This was the favorite engine used by "rum-runners" engaged in smuggling contraband liquor into the United States. Nuta also built some of the finest boats for the trade. Two souped-up Liberty engines on a 34-foot boat could power it to 25 mph when fully loaded, and 45-50 mph if the cargo had to be abandoned. (The liquor was normally packed six bottles to a burlap bag with straw and paper padding, called a "ham." These could easily be thrown overboard, if necessary, and might float until recovered later.) A really fine boat, built from the keel up in Nuta's shop, could cost as much as $14,000 (equivalent to about $250,000 in 1990 dollars).

Boats for this trade also were built at Fogal's Boat Yard and some others. Such boats for the bad guys were sometimes built or serviced side-by-side with Coast Guard boats. (One boat built on the river and photographed near Tracy's Boat Yard during the 1920s had five engines to make it go, but proved to be a bit over-powered and unstable.)

After World War II ended in 1945, Nuta began to develop the Nuta Yacht Basin he had acquired just before the war began. Here boats were built and a full service marina operated with six piers and two lifts. Today this yacht basin, run by Lou Nuta, Jr., includes about 1,300 feet of river frontage.

Adjacent to Nuta's on the upstream side at 21st Avenue is Hardie's Yacht Basin. Richard Hardie established this yard. Richard lived aboard a sturdy two-masted schooner he built himself, assisted by his brother William. Both were sons of Miami's early famous Sheriff Dan Hardie. A third son, Dr. Dan Hardie, was interested and helpful, but occupied with his medical practice. Young Richard planned the yard before World War II, but had to delay completion of it until after his military service in Europe and William's service in the South Pacific (Dr. Dan served in North Africa). Hardie's Yacht Basin was always a first-class place with a true nautical flavor. Richard's idea was that beautiful boats should reside in beautiful surroundings. The yacht basin continues so today, run by a grandson of the same famous name.

An interesting event soon after World War II was the arrival in August and September 1946 of three small sailing vessels carrying 47 Estonian refugees and one Finnish refugee from Europe. These ships were built secretly of trees cut in the forest, launched without being painted, then used to escape from the Russians who occupied their countries. At first these refugees—perhaps Miami's first "boat people"—were confined on Miami's waterfront. Only an order by President Harry Truman prevented their deportation. Miamians gladly provided assistance to the new arrivals. Two of their ships, the *Linda* and *Inanda,* distinguished by their long bowsprits, moved up the river to Hardie's Yacht Basin. They are seen in Figure 16C, resting in the basin as it appeared before its final development after the war.

Figure 16C. Hardie's Yacht Basin, looking north across the river, 1947, (Dan Hardie)

The deep slip at the west end of Hardie's Yacht Basin is leased by Hempstead Marine. Weston Hempstead, Sr. came to Miami in 1921 and worked for Capt. J. O. Webster, who had a yard on the Tamiami Canal near the swing bridge. Among other jobs, they built the jetties at Jupiter and Miami's Government Cut, and blew out Lock No. 1 on the Miami Canal in 1932 when the river and canal were being enlarged. Hempstead towed on the Miami River and Canal during the 1920s and 1930s, taking barges up the canal beyond Hialeah to Pennsuco and the Russian Colony. We are fortunate that Wes Hempstead, Sr. kept a record of his activities and earnings from 1924 through 1935. From it one can observe how he prospered during the Roaring 1920s and suffered during the Great Depression of the 1930s. His experience was typical of many Miamians of that period. (All earnings were translated to modern dollar values for comparison.) Hempstead did well in the early 1920s, and very well as the peak of the boom passed in 1926. His income continued to rise until 1928, when he earned about one third more than early in the decade. In 1929, his income fell to half what it had been the year before, and reached a low in 1933 that was only a fourth what it had been in 1923, and only about one sixth the peak of two years earlier. During those lean years he often turned to work unrelated to the river. By 1935, he was again beginning to prosper, but the Depression was far from over. Many others shared those difficult times.

Wes Hempstead, Sr. and Jr. ran Dunn's Boat Yard (see Chapter 22) before it became Hempstead Marine, and in 1973 moved to a site on the north side of the canal in Hialeah, just above the railroad bridge near 38th Avenue. Operating from that location, their fleet of neat wooden tugboats, white with green trim, were regularly seen on the river. In 1989, they moved downstream to their present location, and in recent years have added several larger steel tugboats to their fleet, most of their work being with the smaller freighters. Wes Hempstead, Jr. and his sons, Norman and Tom, continue to run this well established family business.

Figure 16D. Hempstead Marine tugs with cargo in tow, *Roy* pulling with *Elizabeth* steering the freighter *Key Biscayne*, 1992. (Don Gaby)

Next upstream on the north shore is the Ebsary Foundation Co., formerly part of the Comer-Ebsary Foundation Co. which built the S.W. 2nd Avenue bridge in 1924 and the N.W. 5th Street bridge in 1925—both bridges still in operation today after almost seven decades of faithful service. The Comer-Ebsary Foundation Co. was founded in 1922 to build the new municipal docks, then bulkheaded Bayfront Park before it was filled. (M. F. Comer built the bascule bridges that replaced the original swing bridges at today's Miami Avenue and Flagler Street during the late 1910s.) After the stock market crash of 1929, two companies were formed; Comer near 12th Avenue (their M. F. Comer Bridge & Foundation Co. building is still there in Spring Garden), and Ebsary on North River Drive near 5th Avenue. William H. Ebsary was president with Henry L. Ebsary as secretary-treasurer. William Ebsary continued as president with Richard Ebsary, Sr. as secretary-treasurer until 1975, when Richard Ebsary, Jr. took over.

A project in the early 1930s unrelated to the river was a circular rail track about 900 feet in diameter at Opa Locka, built to carry the mooring mast for the U.S. Navy dirigibles *Akron* and *Macon*. As if to honor the builder, in early January 1933 the *U.S.S. Akron* came south to Miami to help celebrate the fifth annual All American Air Races. Turning in over the Miami River, the giant airship—785 feet long, the world's largest—followed the river up to 27th Avenue, while launching and recovering by trapeze the tiny fighter aircraft carried inside the mother ship. Then she turned north to Opa Locka, coming to rest shackled to the mooring mast on the circular track that allowed her to swing to the wind. (The *Akron* returned to Miami in March, but was lost the following month in a thunderstorm off the coast of New Jersey. Her sister ship, the *Macon*, came in 1934, and the German *Graf Zeppelin* visited later. The *Los Angeles* passed over Miami even earlier, without landing, in 1928. Today, many have forgotten that in the 1920s and 1930s, regular commercial transport service by dirigibles was planned between Europe, South America and the United States, with Miami as a major terminal.)

In the early 1940s, Ebsary moved to its present location near 22nd Avenue. In those days, there was a strawberry field and mango grove in the rich soil of the Allapattah prairie near the site. Ebsary helped build the U.S. Coast Guard base at Government Cut and the seaplane ramp for the Coast Guard (now a public boat ramp) at Dinner Key. The Coast Guard often commandeered their steam derrick to pick airplanes out of the water—it seemed that land-based aircraft from Opa-Locka often could not get their landing gear down and would deliberately land in Biscayne Bay to be picked out with less damage.

Adjacent to the 22nd Avenue bridge on the north shore was Poland's Boat Basin, now called Poland's Yacht Basin. Capt. Jack Poland was a sea captain who used to live at Just's Island and kept his large schooner there (see Chapter 17). Poland was engaged in tramp freighter service between Miami and the West Indies and South America. In 1934, he brought his family to Miami. In the early 1940s, he bought the boat basin property here as a place to keep his boat, digging the slip himself. After retiring from the sea, he dug a lake behind his home in Miami Springs with the idea of making it a marina connected with the Miami Canal. Unfortunately, installation of the salinity dam below 36th Street in 1945 made it difficult and eventually impossible for boats to pass upstream into Miami Springs and Hialeah. Poland's Yacht Basin is run today by Jack's grandson Captain Greg Poland, who took over operations after his father, Pat Poland.

On the South Side of the River

Along most of the south shore we have the Durham Park subdivision of private homes, treated in Chapter 15. The eastern tip was originally a mud flat covered at high tide, but it and much other land was raised with spoil from the river when the Corps of Engineers made it wider and deeper in the early 1930s.

∞

Adjacent to 22nd Avenue, across from Ebsary's and Poland's—before there was a bridge—the famous "Gertie" Walsh (her real name Mary Doleman) had the finest brothel on the Miami River. Gertie had her first place of business on Flagler Street, in the large two-and-one-half-story stone rectory building still standing west of the Dade County Auditorium. That was in George Merrick's Twelfth Street Manors subdivision (Flagler Street was formerly 12th Street), and George might have built Gertie's house. During the boom years of the 1920s, Gertie would dress her "girls" in all

Figure 16E. Gertie Walsh's famous brothel, looking across from the north side of the river, ca.1942. (Roy Neuenschwander)

their finery and parade down Flagler street in an open car. The Flagler Street location may have been too conspicuous for her socially prominent customers. In any case, she moved in the 1930s to this secluded place on the Miami River, with a sparsely settled residential area on one side and undeveloped land on the other. No bridge had yet been built across the north fork of the river at 22nd Avenue.

Gertie's new place was a large two-story house amid lush landscaping that could be reached by automobile or by private yacht. The boat slip seen on the property today was there then. Gertie catered to the wealthy businessmen and politicians of Miami, and to some of its wealthy visitors. Her "girls" were famous for their beauty, and had their Buick and Cadillac convertibles serviced at several nearby gas stations. Gertie's was too expensive for the average man. Among her celebrated customers was William K. Vanderbilt who brought a party of his guests there from Fisher

Island. Another was John D. Hertz, owner of many businesses including the Yellow Cab Company. When in Miami, Hertz had a favorite driver, who on one occasion took him to Gertie's place for three days. The cuisine must have been as good as the girls!

To the regret of many, Gertie Walsh was forced by the Navy to close her establishment during World War II. A friend of the author once helped one of Gertie's girls in a time of need. She offered to return the favor in the best way she knew—but he foolishly declined. The site was abandoned for many years, then planned for a condominium in the 1980s. A serpentine wall built along the south side—a la Thomas Jefferson—indicates that a fine structure was envisioned. This property, just outside of George Marshall's original land grant from President Taylor, was always zoned commercial. Today it is being developed as a shipping terminal and for other uses by the Schurger Diving and Salvage Co. About a dozen venerable oaks from Gertie's old place were saved during construction of this facility.

The present 22nd Avenue bridge, the first to cross the north fork of the river here, was not built by the county until 1966. Like so many others, it is an electrically powered, bascule bridge of four lanes. Unlike some others, it is still young. It is painted orange in accordance with the Miami River Coordinating Committee's "rainbow plan."

Chapter 17
22nd Avenue to Miami Canal Entrance (24th Avenue)

Until after World War I, this stretch of the river on both sides was mostly planted in citrus. It was especially rich soil on the north side. After the war, in 1919, it began to develop for residences when Washburn's subdivision was platted on the north shore west of 22nd Avenue. The steamer *Lady Lou*, a tour boat, brought prospective customers up the river. By the 1920s, there were at least two small yacht basins. These were for the use of upland owners as well as those who held waterfront property.

A famous river character of the early 1930s was the "Bell Ringer of the Miami River." He was just an old guy having a happy time with his hobby. His riverside yard on the north shore by 22nd Avenue was filled with all sorts of gadgets, whirligigs, merry-go-rounds and assorted gew-gaws; all brightly painted in reds, whites, and blues. Many had bells on them, which could be set to ringing by the push of his hand, a pull on a rope, or the turn of a crank. He enjoyed doing this for a little applause from the passengers of the tour boats *Dixie* and *Seminole Queen* as they passed on their way upstream to Musa Isle. Then he'd make a deep bow. The old fellow made the comment, "Once a man, twice a boy." His house is long gone, and the bells, too.

On the north shore near 23rd Avenue we come to Gerry Curtis Park, with a launching ramp for small boats. Originally the Thomas F. Stein tract of 25 acres, the City of Miami acquired it for a park in 1942, and expanded it in later years to 29 acres. It is named in honor of J. Gerry Curtis, a landscape architect and outstanding superintendent of parks who began developing the city's parks, playgrounds and recreation areas in the early 1920s. He served the city for 26 years. Curtis Park once hosted a wide array of high school athletic contests, and today is often used for other activities on the river. A very large improvement of the park for a community sports complex is being completed as this is written. The boat ramp here on the north shore is a convenient place for putting small boats into the river.

On the north shore as we approach the start of the Miami Canal is Just's Island. William G. Just came from Philadelphia in the early 1920s. In 1924, together with T. R. Knight of Miami, he built the El Comodoro Hotel at the northeast corner of S.W. 2nd Avenue and 1st Street, not far from the river. That was one of Miami's finer hotels, with 10 floors, 250 rooms, 250 baths, a roof garden, a coffee shop, etc. That site today is occupied by the Federal Building. About the time the El Comodoro was started, Just also platted the Wm. G. Just subdivision that included Just's Island west of N.W.

24th Avenue and south of 18th Street, plus the two blocks between 24th and 25th Avenues and 18th and 20th Streets. Northwest 24th Court ran between those two blocks and crossed a bridge onto Just's Island. His island was made by excavating a private canal on the north and east sides.

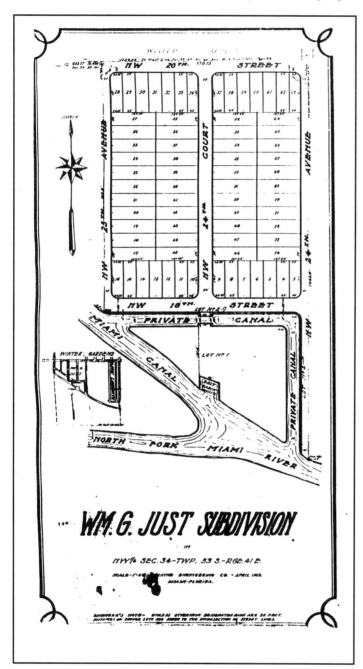

Figure 17A. William G. Just's subdivision, 1923. (Public records of Dade County)

What caused William G. Just to make Just's Island is not known. He built a house on the island in 1925. But he also had a house on two of three lots at the northwest corner of 24th Court and 18th Street, just across from his island, and lived there into the 1940s. In those days the island was connected to the mainland by the bridge at the foot of 24th Court. Quiet and nicely landscaped, Just's Island was formerly a popular place for boaters and river rats. A large boat docked at Just's Island along the main stream side during the 1930s was the three-masted schooner *Ice Field*, built in Nova Scotia, 100 feet on the water, about 140 feet overall, and drawing 8-1/2 feet. She belonged to Capt. Jack Poland (see Chapter 16) who acquired her in Cuba, and used to live on Just's Island. William G. and Ella Just lived on the island in the late 1940s and the 1950s, while a George and Sara Just lived in the home on the mainland. Circumstantial evidence suggests that Just suffered a financial setback when the mid-1920s real estate boom burst. He was retired in the 1960s. Today's modern condominium was built about 1970, at which time bridge access to the island changed from the north to the east side.

On the South Side of the River

The south shore was always more commercial. In the late 1920s, the Fogal Dry Dock and Storage Co. established a second yard at N.W. 24th Avenue and 16th Street Road. (They had their main yard below S.W. 2nd Avenue—see Chapter 7). In February 1928, they completed a broad boat slip and new metal hangar, with 10 feet of water and covering 60,000 square feet. Advertisements guaranteed it would sustain a wind of 150 mph, no doubt with the hurricane experience of 1926 fresh in mind. This became the Florida Yacht Basin, Inc. during the 1940s. It is also known as "The Moorings." During the 1950s, the company expanded to include the property we see today. Hurricane Andrew 1992 tested the "guaranteed" hangar, but not to its full strength; the hanger came through with only minor damage.

We have arrived at Martin's Point, the land situated between the Miami Canal and the north fork of the Miami River. The point is so known for Hugh Martin, who bought the property during World War II and lived on it more than three decades. A sign at the point erected in 1987 directed new arrivals—and some longtime residents—to the left for the river and to the right for the canal—until Hurricane Andrew's passage in August 1992. Next we will follow the very historic Old North Fork of the Miami River.

Figure 17B. Martin's Point with direction sign, river to the left, canal to the right, 1992. (Don Gaby)

Chapter 18
Old North Fork to Former Rapids (29ᵗʰ Avenue)

The north shore of the river in this area west to 27th Avenue was once part of the Watson farm. (See Chapter 19 for an account of that area.) There was an interesting building immediately east of today's 27th Avenue. It was a beautiful square building, board and batten, with a hip shingle roof surmounted by a square cupola-like structure at its peak. A 1901 photograph shows this as an Indian trading post. Perhaps it was established here conveniently near the Everglades to serve those Indians who preferred not to trade in the City of Miami. If so, it would have been built soon after 1896. It appears in photographs of 1913 and later, as in the view from the top of the Cardale Tower below (see Figure 18D).

Figure 18A. Indian trading post below the rapids of the north fork of the Miami River, by today's 27th Avenue, ca. 1901. (Florida State Archives)

In the 1950s, Hugh Martin together with other home owners along the north shore of the river contracted to have the river dredged to about seven or eight feet deep. That dredging ended at about 26th Avenue, beyond which the river has never been dredged and retains some of its original character.

On the South Side of the River

The land immediately on the south shore has long been known as Musa Isle. The first white person to live here was a Seminole War veteran, "Long John" Holman, in 1876. An early "barefoot mailman," in the 1850s he carried the mail down the coast from Fort Capron (near St. Lucie inlet) to Fort Dallas. After the great freezes in the winter of 1894-95, many growers and farmers who had been ruined in northern Florida followed the railroad south to this stretch of the Miami River, to try again in a warmer climate. Among these, the most prominent was Otis Richardson, who settled on the south shore near today's N.W. 25th Avenue.

Two very tall royal palms stand on the south shore across from Martin's Point. These palms appear in a 1907 photograph taken from a tower near the rapids at the headwaters, and even then stood above all of the nearby vegetation—they must be more than a century old. Happily, both survived the passage of Hurricane Andrew 1992. In 1896, Otis Richardson moved here from Bronson, Florida, at the age of 77 and established a grove on the south shore near today's 25th Avenue. His son, C. O. Richardson, joined him the following year; after a career on the stage as an

Figure 18B. Richardson's Grove or the Musa Isle Fruit Farm, on the south side of the north fork east of today's 27th Avenue, ca. 1910. (Historical Museum of Southern Florida)

actor and manager of traveling troupes appearing in the United States and Canada. Father and son developed what became famous as Richardson's Grove. After his father's death in 1901, C. O. Richardson built a tropical preserve and guava products plant, shipping his goods to England and France as well as all over the United States. He changed the name to Musa Isle Fruit Farm, Musa being the botanical name for the bananas that grew at the entrance to the farm. It was the most popular stop up the river for visitors and residents alike. Among his many celebrated guests was Henry Flagler, who visited Musa Isle in 1903 and was quite favorably impressed with Richardson's "patch of bananas." He wrote back from Palm Beach to send a copy of the Nassau Guardian with an article entitled "Cultivation of Bananas" which he had just read.

Figure 18C. C.O. Richardson by his store, ca. 1905. (Historical Museum of Southern Florida)

The severe hurricane of October 1906, that caused so much damage and loss of life on the Overseas Extension of Flagler's Florida East Coast Railway, passed directly over Miami. It did extensive damage to Richardson's grove, uprooting many trees. This was followed by an unprecedented drought in 1907. These two natural disasters marked a turning point for Richardson's Grove (a/k/a Musa Isle Fruit Farm), although it remained a favored tourist stop for several years. Among the tour boats to serve Richardson's Grove were the *Sallie*, the *Lady Lou*, and the *Leo*.

In January 1912, the new Cardale Resort opened at Musa Isle. It had a skating rink and dance floor in a large Quonset-hut shaped building, and an adjoining observatory tower about 90 feet tall right at the edge of the river. For one grand year the Cardale Resort was extremely popular with Miamians who came up the river by the hundreds, by both automobile and boat, to enjoy skating, dancing to a live orchestra, as well as the trip itself. The remoteness of the resort must have been fascinating. That December, a new owner and management offered instruction in both skating and dancing, and announced purchase of a huge Ferris wheel. There was almost no mention of the Cardale Resort after January 1913, and what became of it is a mystery. A photograph taken from the top of the Cardale Tower in March 1913 (Figure 18E) shows a spectacular scene up the Miami River and the newly completed Miami Canal. The large building appears absent by October 1914. An undated postcard showing the Observatory Tower without the large skating rink building is titled "Dr. Thompson's Place near Musa Isle." (Neither Cardale nor Thompson has been identified.) Tommy Carter, a white man who wrestled alligators at the Musa Isle Indian Village begin-

Figure 18D. Musa Isle Fruit Farm (Richardson's Grove) and the Cardale Tower, east of 27th Avenue, ca. l913. (Jack Rabun postcard collection.)

Figure 18E. View toward the west from the Cardale Tower, ca. l913. The Miami River is to the left, the newly excavated Miami Canal to the right. Note the Indian trading post as seen in Figure 18A. (Historical Museum of Southern Florida)

ning in 1932, remembered being told by Sam Willie, a brother of Frank and the famous Willie Willie, that the tall observatory tower simply collapsed. Probably it was the victim of termites or was poorly built, and collapsed well before 1919. The base of the tower lasted into the 1940s.

The Musa Isle Indian Village opened on this site in 1919. Similar to Coppinger's Indian Village downstream at the fork but more commercial, it came to include seven Indian houses or "chickees" with five Miccosukee Indian families in residence during the tourist season. Besides displaying typical Indian life, selling Indian crafts and alligator wrestling, Indian weddings and other functions were staged here. Often the same couples were married more than once, but the tourists loved it, and the cash registers kept ringing. Handling snakes and wrestling alligators were against tribal customs, but the profit motive soon overcame that objection. In the mid-1920s, this tourist attraction was known as "Willie Willie's Seminole Indian Village," Willie Willie being an Indian who had learned the white man's way insofar as making money was concerned. (In the 1920s, Willie also had an "Indian Village" in Hialeah.) Visitors from downtown hotels were brought up the river by boat, or arrived by automobile. During the 1930s and later, both white men and Indians wrestled alligators. This tourist attraction did not close until 1964, and is well remembered by many local residents. Today the site is occupied by the Musa Isle Senior Center, with part of the original rock wall and some old trees still there.

Figure 18F.   Musa Isle Indian Village, ca. 1954.   (Gaby postcard)

ಶಿಂ

Until 1908, there was no bridge on the Miami River above today's Flagler Street. The first bridge to span the north fork crossed here on a county road, today's 27th Avenue, in late 1908. It was one of two bridges promoted by J. C. Baile in connection with the road to "circle the Glades" near Miami (see Chapter 15). It was a fixed wooden bridge, and can be seen in the 1913 photograph from the top of the Cardale Tower. A fixed concrete bridge of two lanes replaced that early bridge in 1916. Another of six lanes replaced it in 1939. A new, higher bridge of six lanes is being built as this is written. It will provide somewhat greater vertical clearance for boats. Historically, many boats, including several large tour boats—much longer than the river was wide—passed upstream west of this bridge.

West of 27th Avenue

The famous rapids or "falls" of the Miami River, which marked its headwaters at the eastern edge of the Everglades, were just two blocks west of today's 27th Avenue. These rapids fell about 6 feet in the course of some 450 feet. Much of that drop took place in the lower portion of the rapids, the flow running into a narrow channel with rocky sides, somewhat lower on the north side. A little east of the rapids was a small stream that ran southwest but has been filled. Just

Figure 18G. Rapids of the north fork of the Miami River, ca. 1900. (Florida News Bureau, Florida State Archives)

below the foot of the rapids was a larger stream that ran north. Beside this stream, called "Ferguson Creek" by the author, the brothers Thomas J. and George W. Ferguson settled with their families in 1845. They built a water-powered starch factory and sawmill over the creek where it makes a bend toward the west, approximately east of the head of the rapids, drawing water from above the rapids to where it was held by a dam, probably built of wood. That same year, Thomas J. Ferguson, Jr. was born—said to be the first white child the Indians had seen. At one time the Fergusons employed 25 people and were very prosperous in the production of coontie or "Arrowroot" starch.

An Indian scare in 1849, together with the discovery of gold in California, caused them to abandon their mill. That year the Army reoccupied Fort Dallas, and stationed a detachment of six men to guard the one man making starch from the Indians. Arthur J. Cooke, the soldier in command, dubbed Ferguson's Mill as "Fort Desolation," and complained about the abundance of mosquitoes and the shaking and noise of the machinery. The Fergusons returned to find their place taken by a brother of former president James L. Polk—a friend of George MacKay who surveyed South Florida after Florida became a state in 1845. Probably the Fergusons had not recorded their land properly, perhaps because that required a difficult journey upstate. Thomas, who struck gold in California, returned home to Baltimore. George began a new operation downriver (see Chapter 12). As late as 1855, the place was still known as "Ferguson's Mill." During the Second and Third Seminole Wars (1835-42 and 1855-58), many military expeditions into the Everglades returned to the Miami River and Fort Dallas here via these rapids.

In July 1896, excavation began for four miles of pipe from a spring-fed pool above the rapids to the young City of Miami at the mouth of the river. The spring water was said to be very soft but with a sulphur taste, to gush three feet above the surface, and to be perceptibly colder (68° F in July) than most nearby springs. Flagler interests decided to provide water for their new city from this spring. They built a pumping station east of the spring and partly over Ferguson Creek (near today's N.W. 21st Street and 29th Avenue). Gasoline engines drove the pumps, and to provide the fuel they built a narrow gauge railway from the north shore of the river to the pumping station. Brought up by boat, the fuel was loaded on a railway handcar and pushed to the pumping station. This arrangement lasted only about one year, after which they moved the pumps downtown to draw rather than push the water to the city. In 1899, to protect the purity of the water, a brick and cement wall about 20 feet across and well above the natural water level was built around the spring to shut out Everglades water.

In 1899, Rev. William H. Phipps, whose brother was with Carnegie and Pops steel manufacturers, visited the site of the old pumping station. He purchased the land east of Ferguson Creek, and by 1902 developed a farm known as "Everglade Edge." Phipps extended the little railway to encircle his farm, evidently returning along the creek to his river landing. By the landing were his warehouse and packing house and a royal palm tree. Three railway cars, with comfortable seats capable of carrying a dozen passengers, were pulled by a powerful black man, George, who was the "whole thing:" conductor, power and all. This was known as the "Everglades Railway." In later years, one railway car was pulled by a mule (see Figure 18H). Visitors could ride to a large house with a second floor observatory room for viewing the Everglades. Because for a short while customers came up to his landing on the tour boat *Leo*, this second floor observatory room became known as the "Leo Observatory." The double-decked *Leo* had to discontinue stops here after the low fixed bridge at 27th Avenue was built in 1908. Today what was the southern part of Everglades Edge Farm is occupied by a mobile home park, a welding shop and the Avalon Restaurant along South River Drive.

Figure 18H. The Everglades Railroad to the Leo Observatory, ca. 1903. (Monroe Collection, Historical Museum of Southern Florida)

Capt. William L. Burch, retired from the Benner Line (see Chapter 6), built the launch *Sallie* just for touring the river. (A second, larger boat of the same name replaced it later.) In 1903, he began regular excursions up the river to the rapids. A first stop might be at Alligator Joe's place near Wagner Creek, a regular stop always was at Richardson's Grove, a/k/a Musa Isle Fruit Farm, and a final stop was near the edge of the Everglades where visitors could view the famous rapids and the 'Glades beyond. For a while, Capt. Burch came to Phipp's landing on the north shore so customers could view the Everglades from his second floor observatory. In 1907, he built his own observatory on the south side just above the rapids. It was a 40-foot tower, reached by a rustic plank walkway from his landing on the south shore just below the rapids. The entire trip cost 25 cents (about six dollars in today's money). It was from this tower that someone made the photograph showing the two royal palms at Musa Isle in 1907. The Burch Tower, also called the Sallie Observatory or Everglades Observatory, can be seen in the 1913 photograph taken from the Cardale Tower—look for the smaller tower above the dip in the tree line appearing directly above the Indian trading post building with its distinctive square cupola (see Figure 18E).

(There was some confusion among early Miamians about the location of this tower. A newspaper article of 1929, long after the tower was gone, stated that this tower was later improved

Figure 18I. Burch's Tower or the Sallie Observatory, ca. 1908. (Historical Museum of Southern Florida)

upon and made higher—and that it was located at "Musa Isle." Since there is no question that Burch's Tower or the Sallie Observatory was built beside the rapids west of today's 27th Avenue, the term "Musa Isle" must have meant that entire parcel of land east of the Everglades and between the forks of the river, the parcel that once was called "Marshall's Island." That would explain why Burch's Tower was also called the "Musa Isle Observatory." What was erroneously described as "later improved upon and made higher," was in fact the entirely different Cardale Tower located east of 27th Avenue.)

Although the Miami River was only 34 feet wide at 27th Avenue, and much more narrow near the rapids, large tour boats like the *Sallie* and *Leo* (well over 40 feet) used to proceed all the way to Burch's and Phipp's landings just below the rapids. From the earliest times, boats drawing as much as four feet could go as far as Ferguson's Creek.

In late 1908, Comfort and Huyler began to dig their canal from the head of the south fork of the river (see Chapter 15) to drain a large tract of land for cultivation, with an option to acquire 50,000 more acres near the head of the north fork. Excavation of the nearby Miami Canal began in May 1909. When it opened in 1912, water levels in the Everglades began to fall and soon the flow of water over the rapids of the north fork ceased. Other springs along the river and in the vicinity soon went dry also. However, as recently as the late 1980s, water continued to trickle out of the ground just above the former rapids. The geologic structure of these rapids was never "dynamited" or removed during construction of the Miami Canal, because that was not needed.

Dade County acquired a parcel of land north of the former rapids to allow constructing a salinity dam and boat lock (see Chapter 21). In 1974, the county gave this land to the City of Miami

Figure 18J. The *Sallie* at Burch's landing, ca. 1910. The plank walkway leads to the "Sallie Observatory" or Burch's Tower. (Gaby, from a slide of unknown origin)

for use as a park. It became Paradise Point Park, and today is the Miami River Rapids Minipark. In recent years, the city acquired use of additional parcels adjacent to the west and eastward to Ferguson Creek. The city also acquired the actual area of the former rapids and designated it archaeological zoning. Perhaps someday this very historic area will be developed as a park, with informative displays to tell its story before there was a City of Miami. Perhaps someday tour boats will again bring visitors right to this park by the former rapids on the Miami River.

Today there are recently completed five-story and 10-story apartment buildings on the south shore just west of 27th Avenue. The absence of boat landings may indicate that the owners are unaware that large boats once routinely proceeded beyond their properties, and down to Biscayne Bay and the ocean.

Chapter 19
Miami Canal (Mainstream), 24ᵗʰ to 27ᵗʰ Avenues

Here by Martin's Point one enters the Miami Canal, mistaken by many for the real river. (Details of the construction of the Miami Canal in connection with Everglades drainage were given in Chapter 2.) Whether draining the Everglades was wise or foolish is arguable. Napolean Bonaparte Broward ran for governor of Florida with a promise to drain the Everglades for agriculture and was elected in 1904. Clearly, draining the Everglades allowed tremendous expansion of greater Miami and other coastal communities, with increased prosperity. The environmental damage and continuing problems it caused were not so easily foreseen then.

Today, much of the agricultural land made available by drainage is poorly used for sod farms and growing sugar cane, and the soil itself is rapidly disappearing by oxidation. Suffice it here to say that the drainage project began in 1906 and that excavation of the Miami Canal began in 1909, with the (still incomplete) canal opened in 1912.

When construction began in 1909, the land north of the river and east of 27th Avenue through which the canal would be excavated was part of the Watson farm. John W. Watson, Sr. came from Kissimmee sometime after 1905, built a home downtown, and established a 20-acre grapefruit grove and farm here. At the south end by the river he raised sugar cane, boiled it and sold the

Figure 19A. Dredge on the Miami Canal, ca. 1911. (Historical Museum of Southern Florida)

syrup. A small frame house and royal palm tree on the north bank of the river seen in early photographs may have been for his caretaker, L. N. Snell. It was good muckland, but after Everglades drainage, Watson said, "you couldn't raise an umbrella." His farm was still there as late as 1921! Watson, Sr. was three times mayor of Miami, a state senator, and 40 years a legislator. (John W. Watson, Jr., for whom today's Watson Island is named, was City of Miami attorney for 30 years.)

Today, the entrance end of the Miami Canal passes through a residential area on the north side. Just's Island was mentioned in an earlier chapter. In 1924, the River Park subdivision was platted between 25th and 26th Avenues. Forty-seven home sites were offered, with 11 lots fronting the canal. Access was from N.W. 20th Street. Of special interest were Lots 4-6 near the foot of 26th Avenue. Here the shoreline was dredged out to accept the "Mori," a large double-decked floating restaurant and cabaret. "Mori of Greenwich Village, New York" opened his "floating restaurant" in January 1925. Johnny Schultz and his Club De Luxe Orchestra provided the music for dancing. Mori advertised his restaurant as being on the "Miami River" at the Musa Isle Bridge. Perhaps he meant to compete with the Silver Slipper on the south fork of the river, also "near Musa Isle." Now the Mori is long gone, but the slip remains in use for private boats.

On the South Side of the River

Hugh Martin came to Miami in 1939 and purchased the pie-shaped piece of land known as "Martin's Point," between the canal and the river and east of a high wall broken only for an entrance way, in 1944. Although formerly farm land, by 1940 it was completely unused, covered by layers of material dredged from the canal with causuarina trees ("Australian pines") getting a start. Martin improved his "point" both as a home and for boat dockage. In about 1950, he floated a house belonging to the mother of his wife Mildred that was on property downstream (today occupied by Kadey-Krogen Yachts, Inc.), up by 27th Avenue, moved it ashore to N.W. 18th Terrace, then rolled it down the street to his place. It was then one of only four houses on that street between the river and the canal. Now improved, it is the larger house with Bermuda roof on the canal side. This land is zoned for commercial use, and is home to many living aboard their boats or houseboats, as well as the Martin children and grandchildren.

To the west of the high wall of Martin's Point is the Paradise Point subdivision, developed in the 1940s, and mostly residential until the 1990s. Of special interest is the second house down from the new 27th Avenue bridge. Former owners added a large, partly-covered porch to connect the house at floor level with the dock. Designed for Florida living and enjoying the river scene, it is the only "river" house that relates to the river or canal in that manner. Much of the yard is planted in native trees—bald cypress, green and silver buttonwood, lyciloma, gumbo limbo, oak, etc. In the front yard is a cannon raised from the *El Infante*, one of the Spanish plate fleet lost in the hurricane of July 1733 soon after leaving Havana. The former owners also removed one section of their dock and many layers of dredged spoil to reveal the original ground.

Figure 19B. River house above Martin's Point, ca. 1989. (Don Gaby)

Figure 19C. "River rat" Lee Luke with Thor in *Driftwood* sailing up the river, ca. 1987. (Don Gaby)

It is interesting to note that whereas this was once productive farm land, equinoctial high tides occasionally rise to flood the original ground level here. Part of the explanation may lie far away. Prior to the making of Government Cut in 1905, there were at least two occasions when strong northwest winds following a cold frontal passage blew much of the water out of north Biscayne Bay, reducing the bay level off the Royal Palm Hotel by several feet and leaving many anchored boats resting on their bottoms. This was never reported after Government Cut was made, nor does it occur today short of a severe hurricane. Probably the easier passage for sea water made it more difficult to lower the bay level, and also increased the tidal range. Opening the cut at Baker's Haulover and increasing the size of Government Cut in later years may have added to the effect.

Also significant today is the stirring of the bottom waters by large tug boats. Years ago the tide was not only less in range, but the more dense salt water tended to lay on the bottom with fresh water above. Barnacles are found growing here today where formerly they were rare or absent.

The county built the first bridge to cross the Miami Canal on 27th Avenue in 1910. It was a single-span wooden drawbridge raised from the south side, constructed perpendicular to the shoreline. The bridge tender's residence was by the southeast corner. The remoteness of the site then may be judged by an incident in March 1912, when the bridge was removed to permit passage of a dredge—the dredge captain transported the mail carrier across the canal in the dredge bucket, to save him a long trip on foot all the way back to the bridge on Flagler Street!

By 1916, the bridge was considered unsafe with the approaches settling. In 1921, a swing-bridge with two lanes, electrically powered but with manual locks, built north-south along the line of 27th Avenue, replaced this early bridge. (This 1921 bridge was removed in 1938 and placed in

Figure 19D. Original N.W. 27th Avenue bridge over the Miami Canal, ca. l910. (Matlack Collection, Historical Museum of Southern Florida)

warehouse storage for use later.) The state provided a temporary bridge upstream while it built today's bascule type, electrically powered, four-lane bridge during 1938-40. Designed by Harrington and Corteyou, consulting engineers from Kansas City, Missouri; construction was by T. A. Loving & Co. of Goldsboro, North Carolina, as a project of the Federal Emergency Administration of Public Works. When it opened in early 1940, many considered it a showpiece of art deco design and modern construction. The bridge approaches were beautifully landscaped, some of the royal palms coming from Coppinger's Tropical Garden downstream. (See Figure 2F for an aerial photograph of this bridge under construction.)

Having served more than half a century, today's 1940 bridge is being replaced with a higher and wider, hydraulically-powered bascule bridge of six lanes. The northbound three lanes are being built as this is written—while the old bridge continues in operation. The Florida DOT donated the former art deco bridge house at the northwest corner (not needed for operations) to the Michael Wolfson Museum of Propaganda and Decorative Arts on Miami Beach. It will be restored, and may be placed on a nearby street. The art deco bridge house at the southeast corner (still needed for operations) may be donated to the Historical Museum for use later in a Maritime Museum. The new bridge will be painted orange to conform with the Miami River Coordinating Committee "rainbow" plan.

This 27th Avenue site is unique in the number and variety of bridges represented. These include a bridge raised from only one side, a swing bridge, bascule-type bridges and bridges powered manually, electrically, and hydraulically. The third bridge to be built on the mainstream of the river system, it will soon be the newest among many.

Figure 19E. Art deco 27th Avenue bridge over the Miami Canal, 1940. (Historical Museum of Southern Florida)

Figure 19F. Art deco bridge house, 27th Avenue bridge over the Miami Canal, 1940. (Historical Museum of Southern Florida)

Chapter 20
27th Avenue to Tamiami Canal Entrance (30th Avenue)

The Miami Canal west of 27th Avenue to the salinity dam near 36th Street is known as the "Second Port of Miami." The vast majority of the cargo leaving the Miami River departs from this area. Although the Miami River and Canal were sufficiently deepened and widened for large deep sea cargo vessels in the early 1930s, development of the port was inhibited by the Great Depression, and by the inadequate bridge at 27th Avenue. Today's 27th Avenue bridge, currently being replaced, was built during 1938-40. Before that time, the bridge used at 27th Avenue was the same bridge now used to cross the Tamiami Canal on South River Drive. Look at that bridge (Figure 21A), just inside the entrance to the Tamiami Canal, and consider how inadequate it must have been for large cargo vessels! Prior to World War II, much scrap metal was barged down the Miami Canal and River to the municipal docks for shipment to Japan. That ended with the Japanese attack on Pearl Harbor that brought the United States into World War II, but today mountains of scrap metal for shipment are still found by the Miami Canal. Development of this section as a port began slowly during World War II.

As recently as 1973, there were only six shipping terminals on the Miami River and Canal, of which Antillean Marine Line (near 31st Avenue on the north side) was the largest. These moved a combined cargo of about 85,000 tons per year. A recent study by the Beacon Council determined that, in 1989, the "Port of the Miami River" served at least 66 shallow draft Caribbean and West Indian ports in 25 countries. There were about 30 shipping terminal operators, who moved about 750,000 tons of cargo valued at $1.7 billion.

This represents a five-fold increase in the number of terminal operators, and a nine-fold increase in cargo carried, in just 17 years. Most of that increase came in the 1980s. Larger ships brought more efficient operations. (Estimated figures for 1990 were one million tons of cargo worth more than two billion dollars!) If the Miami River and Canal were considered as a separate port, it would rank fifth in Florida.

Somewhat typical of these shipping terminals is East River Terminals, across from the entrance to the Tamiami Canal. A Teitelbaum family business, it began in 1937 near today's Metrorail bridge, and relocated upstream near 33nd Avenue in 1940, under the name North River Terminals. The Teitelbaums had their own ships and served Venezuela, Cuba and the Bahama Islands. Poor economic conditions in those countries, plus the drug traffic, caused them to sell their ships and serve as stevedores. In 1989, the company moved downstream to their present larger facility. A fifth generation of Teitelbaums helps Joey Teitelbaum to run this steadily expanding family enterprise.

In the early 1930s, the Osceola Gardens and Indian Village began on a parcel of land between 20th and 21st Streets, running from the Miami Canal east almost to 27th Avenue. (North River Drive—a misnomer—had not been built along this stretch of the canal. For many years, north-bound traffic crossing the Miami Canal on 27th Avenue continued on to the "Buena Vista Road," today's 36th Street, before turning west toward the canal to continue driving northwest along it.) This tourist attraction included a group of Indian "chickee" houses, alligator pens and a dance hall. "Red hot music" and floor shows were advertised. On the Fourth of July 1933, they were selling beer (with little alcohol) and looking forward to the abolition of prohibition soon. By then, 21 states had voted to ratify the 21st Amendment to the U.S. Constitution that would repeal the 18th or "Prohibition" Amendment, and repeal was expected by November. This "Osceola Gardens" did not last long, perhaps being too close to Musa Isle to compete as an Indian Village, and too far from the city for nightlife. In 1936, this area was platted for a residential subdivision.

Adjacent to East River Terminals on the downstream side at 20th Street is a piece of land belonging to Dade County. From this point, a temporary pontoon bridge carried 20th Street traffic across the canal from 1938 into 1940, while the 27th Avenue bridge was under construction. (See Figure 2F.) That pontoon bridge could be moved aside to let boats pass, but in those days the marine traffic was much less. Today, the site is used by the county in part as a dock for the vessel known as *Ms. Clean-Up.*

 In 1964, the county acquired a river clean-up vessel, gathering floating debris and trash five days a week. It was a 36-foot LCVP, a narrow wooden vessel with the well deck about 5-foot deep—that is, well below sea level. It was powered by a single diesel engine, and with a bow ramp designed to be driven ashore on a beach for landing small vehicles and personnel. It was not well suited to the job.

The original effort was inspired and promoted by a very cultivated lady who came to Miami in 1953, and changed her name to Kate Thornhill (it had been Irma LaBastille). LaBastille or Thornhill was a concert pianist, fluent in several languages, a teacher of piano and voice and an author. In the late 1950s, she developed a shipping business on the Miami River below S.W. 2nd Avenue, Kate Thornhill Exports, which engaged in freight forwarding, ship's agent, stevedoring of refrigerated cargoes, livestock and general merchandise. She was one of only a few women in Florida licensed as a stevedore. In 1960, Thornhill became interested in a drive to clean up the river, formed a citizens committee, helped establish the Metro-Miami River Advisory Board, served as its chairwoman for a decade, and in that capacity was most responsible for the county's acquisition of *Ms. Clean-Up.*

In 1973, the county invited bids for a new clean-up vessel. Florida Dredge Industries won the contract with a winning design in 1974. They built a steel boat that was only 34 feet long but much wider, and with the well deck above the water line. It also had a single engine. Put into service in early 1975, it was a much better boat for the job, and continued in operation until August 1991. Negotiations relative to funding as this is written may restore this valuable service.

Figure 20A. *Ms. Clean-Up* at work on the Miami River, 1991. (Don Gaby)

On the South Side of the River

Along the south shore, approximately across from the county's dock, is a large culvert running below South River Drive—another misnomer—and joining the Miami Canal. This is a connection with Ferguson Creek, upon which the Ferguson brothers built their water-powered mill in 1845 (see Chapter 18). It marks approximately the eastern edge of the Everglades before drainage began early in this century. (See the map.) The creek originally ran farther north beyond 20th Street, but that portion has long been filled.

Just upstream from Ferguson Creek, across South River Drive, is the Miami River Rapids Minipark mentioned in Chapter 18. Dade County once acquired the center portion of this park property, but not including the former rapids, plus a narrow strip of land between the park and the canal, to allow constructing a salinity dam and boat lock. In 1946, $2,500,000 (about $25,000,000 in 1990 dollars) was appropriated for a lock and dam just west of 27th Avenue. The Dade County Public Works Department, assisted by the U.S. Army Corps of Engineers, planned a permanent salt water barrier at this location. It was still planned in 1955. In 1962, a Planning Study of the Miami River, by the Metropolitan Dade County Planning Department, continued to recommend such a structure, and a model of the Salinity Control Dam and Navigation Locks proposed by the Public Works Department was prepared. In 1966, the U.S. Geological Survey, under contract to the State of Florida, made a Salt-Water Study of the Miami River and Its Tributaries. Their study

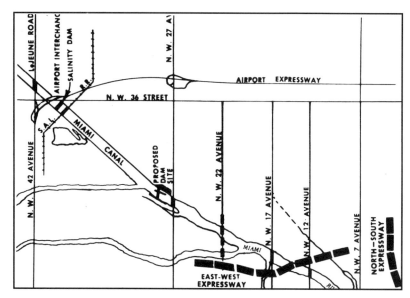

Figure 20B. Map of proposed salinity dam and boat lock location, ca. 1962. (Adapted from map by Dade County Public Works Department, Metro-Dade Public Library)

showed that the existing salinity control structure on the Miami Canal appeared inadequate to prevent the intrusion of salt water into Miami's fresh water well fields. A suggested solution still was to install a salinity dam and lock for boats downstream from the confluence of the Miami and Tamiami Canals, that is, at this location.

An alternative solution to the problem of salt water intrusion was found: 1) by improving the salinity control structure on the Miami Canal near 39th Avenue, 2) building salinity control structures on the Tamiami Canal near 40th Avenue and on the Comfort Canal at its entrance near 28th Avenue, and 3) developing new well fields farther south and west. With increasing population and demand for fresh water, it remains to be seen whether someday the proposed dam and lock for boats will be needed. In any event, Dade County gave this property to the City of Miami in 1974 for use as a park. Additional land on both sides of the original park was acquired in the late 1980s for expansion of that park. The large building seen in the park near Ferguson Creek is the recently completed The Miami Bridge, a home for runaway teenagers.

Figure 20C. Model of Salinity Control Dam and Navigation Locks on the Miami Canal above N.W. 27th Avenue, ca. 1962. (Dade County Public Works Department, Metro-Dade Public Library)

Chapter 21
Tamiami Canal to Salinity Dam (40ᵗʰ Avenue)

A highway to cross Florida through the Everglades from Miami to Tampa was proposed in 1915. It was called the Tamiami Trail. Construction of that highway required a canal from which to obtain road fill. An early plan called for the highway to parallel the Miami Canal to its junction with the South New River Canal, then proceed westward via Immokalee. The final route which we know today crosses the Everglades much farther south, and enters Miami on S.W. 8th Street. Work began in 1916, but World War I and many unforeseen construction problems delayed its completion until 1928.

An almost forgotten piece of local history is that in September 1917 the State of Florida entered into a contract with J. H. Tatum and associates, who proposed to build a railroad line from Miami to Tampa. The trustees of the Internal Improvement Fund (IIF) agreed to sell certain rights-of-way on state lands to Tatum (on a mortgage) at $500 per mile. That railroad was to run on or near the banks of the Miami Canal, and be standard gauge. Payments on the mortgage were to be completed by December 1924, or sooner, if the railroad was completed sooner. Construction was to begin no later than February 1918. Failure was not long in coming. What difficulties were encountered are not known, but the IIF trustees released Tatum from the mortgage in August 1919 and his railroad was never built.

Tatum's proposed railroad to Tampa would come up from the south, cross the Tamiami Canal where it joined the Miami Canal, then follow the south side of the Miami Canal until it crossed the canal into Hialeah (Miami Springs had not yet arrived). Then it would follow the north side of the Miami Canal to pass around the east side of Lake Okeechobee, etc. By the 1920s, another railroad was proposed. It also would come from the south to cross the Tamiami Canal, then run west along the north side of the Tamiami Canal to the west coast. Neither proposed railroad was built.

In August 1919, the state approved a drainage canal to connect the new Tamiami Canal with the Miami Canal. Jesse L. Megathlin, of the Megathlin-Clark Dredging Co., made the connection by the end of that year. Some work may have been done earlier by W. R. Comfort, a New York millionaire candy manufacturer, who was draining and developing a huge acreage in that area for sugar cane production (see Chapter 15). The connecting canal appears to have been called the "Comfort Canal" after W. R. Comfort; it was also called the "Connecting Canal," and the "Crosscut Canal." In April 1920, a dredge in the Miami River was brought up to enlarge the new canal. What is known today as the Tamiami Canal, where it joins the Miami Canal, was made in 1920, although part of the excavation from the east end was completed much earlier.

Turning into the Tamiami Canal from the Miami Canal, one immediately comes to a swing bridge. The earliest bridge here on today's South River Drive (a misnomer) was a "country bridge" built in 1915. It crossed a narrow natural stream, and was a fixed wooden bridge to serve farmers working the land to the northwest. In 1918, by which time a canal was started, a manually operated, one-lane swing bridge was installed when the "military road" to the U.S. Marine Corps

Flying Field was improved. A residence for the bridge tender was nearby. The two-lane swing bridge used from 1921 into 1938 to cross the Miami Canal on 27th Avenue, taken from warehouse storage, replaced that early swing bridge during World War II. This bridge was electrically powered, but with manual locks. In recent years, it has been renovated and improved. Serving in two locations for almost seven decades, this is the oldest bridge on the Miami River system.

Figure 21A. The oldest bridge on the Miami River system, this swing bridge presently on the Tamiami Canal at South River Drive previously served on the Miami Canal at 27th Avenue, 1990. (Don Gaby)

Proceeding up the Tamiami Canal, there are several boatyards and other marine related businesses, as well as many private homes. Perhaps most noteworthy among the businesses is the Bertram Yacht Corp. Richard Bertram pioneered the deep-vee hull design after winning the 1960 Miami to Nassau powerboat race in heavy seas. Bertram founded the company in Hialeah, but moved to the present location on the north side of the Tamiami Canal just east of 37th Avenue in 1962. The manufacturing plant is across the street. Today, Bertram boats are famous and found around the world.

Beyond the fixed bridge at 37th Avenue, a quiet stretch of the Tamiami Canal borders the municipal Mel Reese Golf Course on the south shore. The Sheraton River House Hotel, on the north shore, is a recent addition from the 1970s. Just beyond, at about 40th Avenue, is a salinity control structure installed in late 1971. It marks the end of navigation today. However, the Tamiami Canal continues on through Blue Lagoon Lake, south of Miami International Airport, where it is joined by the Comfort Canal running from the head of the south fork of the river.

Chapter 22
Miami Canal, Tamiami Canal to Palmer Lake Entrance (34th Avenue)

Many of the larger shipping terminals and other marine businesses are located along both sides of this portion of the Miami Canal. As already mentioned, most of these began after World War II.

On the north shore near 33rd Avenue, adjacent to the former lock on the Miami Canal, there was a large steel warehouse for storing used newspapers during the 1930s. It burned in 1940. Later that year the Teitelbaums established their North River Terminals on this site. In 1989, the company moved downstream with a change of name to East River Terminals (see Chapter 20).

Directly across from today's Jones Boat Yard and the entrance to Palmer Lake, Lock No. 1 of the Miami Canal and an associated dam were located. The state's contractor excavating the Miami

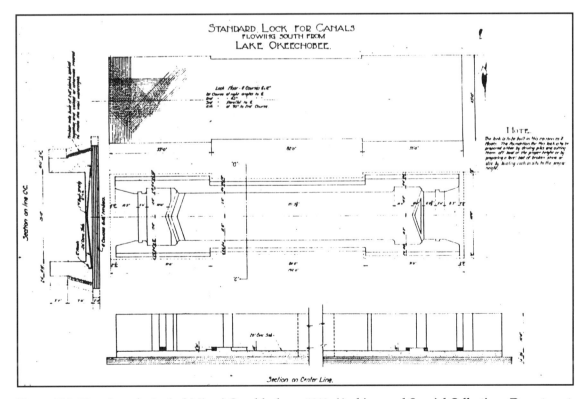

Figure 22A. Drawing of a typical Miami Canal lock, ca. 1912. (Archives and Special Collections Department, Richter Library, University of Miami)

Canal built a temporary earthen dam just above this location in 1910 to contain sufficient water to float their dredge. The state planned a boat lock and permanent dam as early as 1911, but did not complete it until late 1912. Built of reinforced concrete with wooden doors, it had interior dimensions 121 feet long and 25 feet wide, designed to pass barges or boats of almost that size drawing as much as 3-1/2 feet of water. (Today a similar lock may be seen at the State Historic Site at the north end of the Miami Canal, just south of U.S. Highway 27 near Lake Okeechobee.)

Poor control of the lock in the early years often caused as much flooding of the surrounding farms as it was meant to control. This was sometimes by neglect, but as often deliberately to prevent cheaters from passing through the open lock without paying their tolls. Tolls for farmers hauling produce were eventually removed.

The dam beside Lock No. 1 was removed in about 1921, allowing a free flow of water. In October 1929, to relieve flooding in Hialeah and the Country Club Estates (today's Miami Springs), the state removed the lock's heavy doors in an effort to allow a more free flow of water. Finally, in 1932, Capt. J. O. Webster, subcontractor, with Weston Hempstead, Sr., blasted out the concrete portions of the old lock during the deepening and widening of the Miami River and Canal by the U.S. Army Corps of Engineers.

On the South Side of the River

Among the early businesses on the south side was Dunn's Boat Yard near 33rd Avenue (south side avenues do not align with north side avenues in this section). William S. Dunn had a boat house and livery here as early as 1927. He expanded and began Dunn's Boat Yard in 1929. Weston Hempstead, Sr. came to run the yard in 1942, making many improvements and greatly expanding the yard. Dunn's Boat Yard won a contract to maintain the air rescue boats from Homestead Army Air Field (today's Homestead Air Force Base) during World War II. Weston Hempstead, Jr. took over the yard in 1962, running it for another decade. He changed the name to Hempstead Marine, but many boaters continued to use the older name. It was both a full service and do-it-yourself yard, very popular among many of Miami's boaters. In 1973, the yard was sold to another party, and Hempstead moved his business across the canal and upstream (see Chapter 16). For several years, the old yard was in decline, until Transcaribbean Shipping purchased the property. In recent years, this site has been occupied by Bernuth Marine, one of the larger shipping terminals on the Miami Canal.

Glenn H. Curtiss, an aviation pioneer with many interests, established a flying school in January 1917 on land leased from the Bright Bros. Ranch, in today's Hialeah, several miles up the canal on the north side. In May, the Curtiss Flying School moved to a permanent site where Jones Boat Yard is today. Curtiss may have selected that site, just below the lock and dam, for the convenience of not having to transit the lock. Here the school trained both Army and civilian pilots. Curtiss constructed a large building as an assembly hangar for aircraft, and for storage of speedboats from his Curtiss Exhibition Co. An unpaved runway ran east to west from the canal. He dredged a boat slip to facilitate the delivery of fuel and removal of the speedboats. Curtiss intended to use the facility for his fast watercraft as well as for aviation training. A narrow road along the south side of the Miami Canal led to the flying school.

Figure 22B. U.S. Marine Corps Flying Field adjacent to Lock No. 1 with dam on the Miami Canal, looking west, 1919. (Matlack Collection, Historical Museum of Southern Florida)

By the time the United States entered World War I in April 1918, a U.S. Marine Corps Flying Field was established on the site, Curtiss leasing the land to the government for that purpose. Soon a large military complex developed with hangars, storehouses, machine shops, tent camps and gunnery and bombing ranges. Pilots for four squadrons trained here, plus gunners, mechanics and other ground crew. Most of the pilot training was in the famous Curtiss "Jenny" aircraft, but various others were used as well. (Among those training as a mechanic was a pioneer Miamian, Charles David Millard, brother-in-law of Cleveland H. Jones, Sr., who later founded Jones Boat Yard on the site.) These four squadrons made up the 1st Aviation Force, vanguard of Marine aviation in the war zone.

All four squadrons saw service in France during World War I. Twenty-two pilots were killed in combat, in addition to at least 10 killed here while training, plus other pilots and support personnel who died of sickness both here and overseas. In all there were 57 dead from this short but intensive period of training and service. After the Armistice in November, these units were returned promptly, and by August 1919 the field was abandoned by the military. Some flying may have continued at the field into 1921.

Cleveland H. Jones, Sr., a yacht captain, acquired the portion of the former airfield that fronted the Miami Canal in 1922. It included 210 feet of water frontage, and the boat slip made by Glenn Curtiss. (It also included a pile of old aircraft wreckage and parts. Later, Jones found a Lewis machine gun in the canal while dredging a basin.) Here he built a house, located where today we find the basin for two floating dry docks of the Jones Boat Yard. In the early 1920s, Jones rented his house, the boat slip and dock space to the Caraway Boat Co. The famous 1926 hurricane destroyed

Figure 22C. Marine Flying Field bombing office, 1919. (Matlack Collection, Historical Museum of Southern Florida)

Figure 22D. Marine Corps scout and bombing aircraft, ca. 1918. (Matlack Collection, Historical Museum of Southern Florida)

the house. During the late 1930s, Jones had the original Curtiss boat slip enlarged and deepened to make a rectangular basin, to which he added a hangar in 1956. In 1940, he made a new basin upstream, which today is covered by a large hangar added in 1978.

Cleve Jones, Jr. took over management of the Jones Boat Yard in the mid-1950s. The company acquired the property on the opposite side of the entrance to Palmer Lake in 1980, and the following year acquired the channel itself that leads to Palmer Lake. Jones, Jr. expanded their operation on the property upstream across the channel to Palmer Lake, and added the large hangar and the floating dry docks mentioned above. Always a family operation, the Jones Boat Yard, after more than half a century, has grown to include 1,200 feet of water frontage, the only dry docks on the lower east coast of Florida, and the largest hauling capacity in the area. Famous vessels serviced in recent years include the research submarine *Alvin*, the presidential yacht *Julie*, the Chicago Blackhawks' 123-foot yacht *Blackhawk*, and Ralph Evinrude's 118-foot yacht *Chanti-cleer*.

Figure 22E. Jones Boat Yard with a variety of craft for servicing, ca. 1983. (Don Gaby)

Chapter 23
Palmer Lake

Palmer Lake is artificial, excavated in part from where the runway for the Curtiss Flying School and U.S. Marine Flying Field was located. The George H. Palmer Co. began excavating Palmer Lake in the mid-1920s, and continued until the 1926 hurricane. In the early 1930s, Palmer leased the property to the Destin Sand and Rock Co. Alfred Destin had a ready-mix concrete plant here on the lake, with an office downriver just north of where Jose Marti Park is today. Rock was brought to the plant from Maule Lake (today part of Blue Lagoon Lake). Barges used to take sand and rock down the river and elsewhere. In the late 1940s, Destin bought the property, then sold it to Maule Industries in the early 1950s. Maule brought rock from their Maule Lake to the plant on Palmer Lake. Later they filled part of the lake for an industrial park, but about 20 acres remain.

The Act of Congress of 3 July 1930 that authorized the deepening and widening of the Miami River and Miami Canal also included provision for "a channel 12 x 100 feet from Miami River to a harbor of refuge in Palmer Lake or other suitable location." The original entrance to Palmer Lake was a dogleg channel made to avoid private property. The Army Corps of Engineers straightened that short channel from the Miami Canal to Palmer Lake, but did not make it to the authorized dimensions. The fixed bridge on South River Drive, crossing this short canal leading to the lake, blocks the entry of sailboats or powerboats needing much vertical clearance.

Whether officially so designated or not, Palmer Lake has served occasionally as a harbor of refuge for small boats during hurricane events. It is also a refuge for manatees and other marine animals.

Figure 23A. Hurricane warning flags flying on the Miami River. (NOAA National Hurricane Center)

Chapter 24
Miami Canal, Palmer Lake Entrance to Salinity Dam (35ᵗʰ Street)

This final stretch of our journey takes us to the end of navigation on the Miami Canal. There are several shipping terminals and other marine businesses on both sides of the Miami Canal. Most of these began well after World War II.

An early business is Auto-Marine Engineers, established in 1934 by Plato Cox, known as "the Old Man of the Miami River." Cox came to Miami as a child in 1911, after his grandparents who had sailed down before the turn of the century. He started his business on Biscayne Boulevard in the early 1930s. In the late 1930s, Cox took a partner and moved down on the river at 451 N.W. North River Drive, advertising auto and boat repairs. During the 1940s, he became the distributor for Buda diesel engines. Cox also acquired river property downstream on the south side—lost when the city acquired it for Jose Marti Park. In 1952, he moved the business upriver to its present location on the north side of the Miami Canal near 35th Avenue. Plato Cox ran his business on the river for some 15 years, and here on the canal for another 34 years, selling and repairing diesel ship engines primarily. His ability to locate difficult-to-find parts or engines was legendary. Plato Cox's presence on the "river" covered half a century. The business he started continues under the direction of his daughter, Joy Hooper.

A recent addition is Miami River Recycling, on the north side near 37th Avenue, established here in 1990. Wrecked automobiles and "white ware" (large appliances), are reduced to very small pieces that can easily be moved and handled. It is a "water-dependent" operation because of the need to transport the processed scrap by barge to larger vessels.

The Seaboard Air Line Railway Co. ran trains between Miami and New York as early as 1916, but not on their own tracks. For many years the company planned to extend its own tracks to Miami. In March 1926, the City of Miami gave the company the right-of-way for tracks along North River Drive between 23rd and 37th Streets (31st to 40th Avenues). That September, the Seaboard crossed the Miami Canal on a temporary wooden draw bridge at 36th Avenue, southeast of the new Biscayne Fronton. Their first freight train arrived at Miami in December. In January 1927, their famous Orange Blossom Special passenger train arrived. Today's single-track, single-bascule, steel railroad bridge, upstream on a line with 38th Avenue, was completed later.

Figure 24A. Miami River Recycling plant and barges on the Miami Canal, 1992. (Don Gaby)

ॐ

Just above the railroad bridge, a small part of the City of Hialeah reaches the north bank of the Miami Canal. It is known as the "Port of Hialeah." Until 1940, boats could proceed easily into Hialeah itself.

ॐ

As one approaches the end of navigation on the Miami Canal, there is a "step" in the hard bottom several hundred feet below the salinity control structure near 35th Street. Here the depth of the hard bottom decreases about four feet, marking where the Corps of Engineers began their massive dredging operation in 1932.

ॐ

The danger of salt water intrusion into the Everglades drainage canals was recognized as a potential problem before the Everglades drainage project began early in this century. The boat lock and dam on the Miami Canal near 34th Avenue, mentioned in Chapter 23, were removed in the early 1920s and 1930s. By 1940, the state built a tidal gate below 36th Street of sheet steel piling, used during parts of 1940 and 1943-46. They installed a leaky sheet metal dam there in 1946. A mechanical lift provided for moving boats to 45 feet and 20 gross tons over the dam. That salinity control structure was much improved about 1970.

Among the last boats to attempt the crossing in the 1960s was the *Lizzie Pettigrew*, a former sailboat of about 60 feet and 12 tons powered by a huge single-cylinder gasoline engine. This engine, firing at long intervals, made a very distinctive sound, which was recognized on the river long before the boat came into view. Christian Mortensen, her captain, lived down the bay and would come upriver occasionally to fill his water barrels at the water plant in Hialeah. It was a sight to see! The boat was still fitted with a tiller, and the captain steered from the bow while leaning against two lines running aft to the tiller. The *Lizzie Pettigrew* was dropped on the salinity control structure when the lifting machinery failed! She is well remembered by many old-timers on the river.

Figure 24B. The last voyage of the *Lizzie Pettigrew*, dropped on the salinity control structure below 36th Street, ca. 1965. (Newspaper photograph, Dan Hardie)

Epilogue

The author hopes the reader has enjoyed his or her journey up the Miami River and its tributaries, and has learned something along the way. Although the once wild and beautiful river of previous centuries is now but a memory, the river is very much alive.

Many Miamians still live on the river and the future should see still more. Several parks preserve some of the original natural beauty, while providing the public direct access to the river. Riverwalks in the downtown area, and new buildings that strive to improve the beauty of the river's shores are but the beginning of an effort to revitalize our river. As this is written, there is serious discussion of a Performing Arts Center on the north shore near the Metrorail crossing— and of a Miccosukee Indian/Historic Village in Lummus Park. Who can imagine what other improvements may be added?

Today's Miami River is a "working river," and therein lies much of its charm and interest. Both residents and visitors enjoy watching this commercial traffic to and from many foreign ports. The commerce adds much to the economy and prosperity of the community.

As more of the people in Miami and Dade County come to appreciate the vital importance of the river system to the condition of Biscayne Bay and a healthy environment, more community support for needed improvements may be expected. The future is indeed bright, and one may envy the historian who will be able to recount that future.

About the Book's Sponsors

Merrill-Stevens Dry Dock Co.

Spanning five generations, Merrill-Stevens Dry Dock has established an extraordinary history of quality and service in the marine field. The beginnings of today's impressive operation are humble, indeed. Captain James Gilman Merrill originally opened a small blacksmith shop along the shores of the St. Johns River in 1866. Located in Jacksonville, Florida, the leading deep-water port in Florida at the time, the small blacksmith shop grew considerably during the next 10 years, operating as an ironworks primarily serving the marine trade. The company was formally incorporated in 1885 by James Eugene Merrill, making Merrill-Stevens Florida's oldest continuously operating company. Merrill-Stevens expanded into Miami in 1923.

Into the early 1900s, Merrill-Stevens kept pace with Florida's booming growth. A publication of that period described the company, then managed by James Eugene Merrill, as an "immense shipyard and dry docks visited by vessels from practically every port in the world." The second-generation ownership invested an enormous sum of money at the time in the company to develop the yard's capacity to accommodate ships up to 4,500 tons. It was an investment that paid off, as the company prospered through the Spanish-American War and World War I. This investment also allowed the company to weather periods of major setbacks, including two depressions, a devastating north Florida freeze, the cataclysmic Jacksonville fire of 1901, which reduced the shipyard to charred pilings and twisted metal, and the 1992 record destruction of Hurricane Andrew.

By the time World War II broke out, Merrill-Stevens had grown to become the largest Atlantic shipyard south of Norfolk, Virginia, with dry docks capable of lifting 12,000-ton ships in a half-hour. The third-generation chief executive of Merrill-Stevens, James Campbell Merrill, founded the St. Johns River Shipbuilding Co., which delivered 82 Liberty ships to the U.S. Maritime Commission and a dozen 3,500-ton tankers to the U.S. Navy. During the war, more than 2,000 commercial and military vessels were repaired or refitted at Merrill-Stevens.

Merrill-Stevens Dry Dock Co., 1993.

Florida Marine Towing Co., Inc.

Florida Marine Towing specializes in towing ships in the Miami River. This operation has evolved through the decades with the towing during the company's first 30 years done primarily by Backus Towing Co.

The Miami River is unique in the entire maritime world in its operations: the ships are towed as dead ships up the river, head first, and out loaded, stern first. Shipmasters and tug operators from all over the world have commented that the skill levels of the tug operators are among the highest. It is not unusual for tug operators to negotiate through passages with inches to spare.

During the 1960s and '70s, the ships were small, 200-foot or less, and shallow draft. The tugs were small with low horsepower. During the 1980s, however, the ships grew larger and loaded deeper. Backus Towing responded by building two 800 horsepower, 52-foot tugs. These twin screw tugs were built especially for the river. Typical towing tugs at the time were single screw and around 300 horsepower.

Florida Marine Towing began in the bunkering business in 1985, and purchased larger tugs, 70 foot, 1,000 horsepower and 1,800 horsepower, to handle the bunkering barges. In 1986, the business expanded in the river as Backus Towing became overloaded and the ships continued to grow, requiring larger tugs. In 1987, Florida Fuels shifted their bunkering business to ships instead of barges, and Florida Marine Towing then became an exclusive river towing company.

In 1990, Backus Towing was sold to Florida Marine Towing, and the three smaller tugs were sold off. The towing tugs were then 800 horsepower and tail tugs 1,000 to 1,800 horsepower

In 1989, ships were brought to the Miami River that were bordering on the maximum size the river could accommodate. At the time of this publication, 10 vessels call to the river terminals that are 300-feet long with beams to 52 feet. These vessels are capable of carrying 3,500 to 4,000 tons. Florida Marine Towing places a lookout on the ships to assist the tug captains, and has required all vessels over 275 feet to have bow thrusters to assist the tugs in maneuvering.

Operators of the terminals and ships, along with Florida Marine Towing, have kept pace with technology and environmental concerns with safety always the uppermost consideration. Although the future of the Miami River has many uncertainties, the prospect of both the Haitian and Cuban embargoes being withdrawn means vessel and cargo traffic could boom at any time.

Biscayne Bay Pilots Association

Since 1911, pilots of the Biscayne Bay Pilots Association (which until 1969 was known as the Miami Bar Pilots) have ensured the safe movement of both cargo and cruise vessels in and out of the Miami River and the Port of Miami.

The Biscayne Bay Pilots Association operates from their modern pilot station, opened in 1989 at the east end of Lummus Island. The boarding station is about 3-1/2 miles offshore with the pilotage in or out of the Miami River and/or the Port of Miami typically taking 1-1/2 hours.

The pilot's job is exacting and highly responsible, requiring precise skills and an exhaustive depth of knowledge and training. In colonial America, piloting had been an important, highly regarded profession. Today, pilot applicants must possess merchant marine experience as a ship's officer or captain, plus additional qualifications via the U.S. Coast Guard examination station in order to sit for the Florida State Pilots Examination.

Only after achieving the highest scores on an extensive series of U.S. Coast Guard and State of Florida tests is a pilot accepted as a deputy pilot in training. The path for would-be pilots is further narrowed by the fact that most pilots remain in service for their entire career and because pilots may not be added unless the Florida Board of Pilot Commissioners deems more are necessary to handle increased port traffic. Pilots in Miami are specialists with this port only.

According to state law: "The legislation recognizes that the waters, harbors and ports of the state are important resources, and it is deemed necessary in the interests of public health, safety and welfare to provide laws regulating the piloting of vessels utilizing the navigable waters of the state in order that such resources, the environment, life and property may be protected to the fullest extent possible."

The pilots must cope with such routine hazards as limited water depths for deep-draft vessels, hard coral reefs and banks, shifting currents, inclement and increasingly heavy overall ship traffic through Government Cut. The pilots also handle emergency duties, such as the clearing of ships from port in the event of a close-out order issued by the Coast Guard due to an approaching hurricane.

Miami River Marine Group

The Miami River Marine Group is a not-for-profit corporation committed to harnessing resources to help assure that the Miami River remains a *working river*. The Group's activities focus on marketing, public relations, advocacy, education and promotion toward building continued support for Miami River awareness and for the marine industry's economic vitality.

Eighteen shipping terminals transport more than one million metric tons of cargo with a valuation of over $2 billion every year from the Miami River. The Dade County portion of the river (west of the 27th Avenue bridge) is home port to ocean freighters destined for 67 ports in the Caribbean, and to Central and South America. This activity generates over $200 million to South Florida's economy, with cargo volume increasing at a rate of 15 percent annually. Some 8,000 direct full-time jobs are connected to the Miami River industry.

The Miami River Marine Group works to promote the continuation of this commercial shipping activity. Specifically, the Group strives to educate the public and all levels of government about critical decisions affecting the Miami River as a major port for commercial cargo in Florida; to promote a positive image of businesses on the Miami River by encouraging practices in the best interest of the River's economic and environmental health; and to organize corporate, community, and governmental resources to make commercial shipping goals a reality.

Founded in 1989, member corporations in the Miami River Marine Group include: Antillean Marine Shipping Corp., Bernuth Agencies, Inc., Bunnell Foundation, Coastal Tug & Barge, Inc., East River Terminals, Inc., Florida Marine Towing Co., Inc., Hyde Shipping Corp., International Maritime, S.A., Jones Boatyard, Mesa Marine Repairs, Miami Ship Services, Inc., Miami Shipyards Corp. and Schurger Diving & Salvage.

Teo A. Babun, Jr.

Teo A. Babun, Jr. is carrying forth his family's tradition in which the Miami River has played an important role. Teo's father, Teofilo "Tofi" Babun, was president of Antillean Marine Shipping Corp. and other businesses he began up and down the river. He came from Cuba to Miami at the time of Castro's takeover and remained a patriot working to advance the cause of freedom in his homeland until his death.

Teo Babun, Jr. continues to live out his father's legacy of starting over and rebuilding. He formed Cuba/USA Venture Enterprises, a company preparing to bring business to a free Cuba. He carries forth the vision of a free Cuba in honor of his father's name.

Active in the community and often sought-after as spokesman on the Miami River and many other topics important to South Florida, Teo Babun, Jr. has a vision for a maritime museum in Miami — with the Miami River a prominent component. He is working with the Historical Association of Southern Florida for such a museum, in which Miami's rich maritime heritage will be documented, preserved and exhibited for generations to come.

Teo Babun, Jr. currently holds top positions in several South Florida companies, such as president and chief executive officer of the T. Babun Group, Inc.; chairman of Babun Shipping Corp. and president of Maritima Services Co.

Teo Babun, Jr. has taken a leadership role in a wide-ranging array of civic organizations. Among business and international affairs positions, he serves on the executive committee of the Greater Miami Chamber of Commerce, as vice-chairman of the City of Miami International Trade Board, as chairman of the Cuba Trade Preparation Committee and on the executive committee of the World Trade Center in Miami.

Teo A. Babun, Jr. has worked extensively to improve the Miami River both in ecological and commercial aspects. He founded the Miami River Marine Group and serves as chairman of Citizens for Arts and the River.

Walter R. Ferguson

Walter R. Ferguson is a sixth generation North Carolinian who moved to Miami with his family as a boy in the early 1930s. He fell in love with the Miami River in his youth and has been involved with the river ever since.

Soon after the family's arrival, Walter Ferguson lived on a boat named *New Deal* which was moored between Flagler and Fifth Streets. He spent his boyhood summers as a crew member on two- and three-masted sailing schooners and freighters in Caribbean trade. The *Helen May Schocht, Ice Field* and *Josephine Whimsett* are some of the vessels for which he crewed in his youth.

In 1951 after training in the U.S. Coast Guard Merchant Marines, he established Southern Diesel Engine Repair, a thriving business near the river at 244 S.W. 6th Street. Over the years, he became affectionately known as the "Mayor of Sixth Street."

Walter Ferguson retired in mid-1993 to continue to enjoy South Florida and its waterways. In his spare time—when he is not busy overseeing the vineyards on his island in the Caloosahatchee River—he can be seen at the helm of his vessel, the *Florida Queen,* a 21-foot steam launch.

The Publisher: The Historical Association of Southern Florida

The Historical Association of Southern Florida operates one of the largest private, regional history museums in the country. Founded in 1940 as a non-profit corporation and accredited by the American Association of Museums since the late 1970s, the museum's tradition of excellence was awarded the #1 ranking among Florida's largest art, history and science museums in 1993.

The museum is located in the heart of Miami just north of the Miami River in the Metro-Dade Cultural Center. The museum produced an exhibition on the Miami River in its state-of-the-art facility in 1987, and in 1990 published Don Gaby's pocket guide for the Miami River.

Because of the historical significance of the Miami River to the community, the Historical Association sought to publish this more comprehensive work on the river as part of its ongoing publications program. Other publications include an annual scholarly journal published since 1940, *Tequesta,* the popular history quarterly, *South Florida History Magazine,* a membership newspaper, *Currents,* and a periodic series of exhibition catalogs, books and historical reference works.

The association operates extensive educational programs that take place both in the museum and as outreach programs. The museum is noted for its exciting and participatory approaches to the exploration of history and every year serves students from age 3 to adult. Tours of the Cape Florida Lighthouse, the Everglades and the Miccosukee Indian Village, and boat trips to historically significant South Florida waterways such as the Miami River are among the many stimulating programs provided.

The Historical Association of Southern Florida is governed by a Board of Trustees and is operated by 22 full-time professional staff members and 15 part-time educators and operations personnel. More than 500 volunteers give their time annually in nearly every area of the institution.

Select Bibliography

Books

Bonawit, Oby J., *Miami Florida—Early Families and Records*, manufactured in the U.S.A., 1980.

Elliott, Andrew, *Journal of Andrew Elliott* (done 1799, published 1803?).

Florida, The East Coast, edited and published by *The Miami Herald*, Miami, undated, circa 1925.

Giddings, Joshua R., *The Exiles of Florida*, Follett, Foster and Company, Columbus, Ohio, 1858.

Huff, Van E. & Robert Hardin, *From Mountains to Miami*, The Franklin Press, Miami, 1982.

Johnson, Clifton, *Highways and By-ways of the South*, MacMillan, 1904.

Mahon, John K., *History of the Second Seminole War, 1835-1842*, Revised Edition, University of Florida Press, Gainesville, 1985.

McIver, Stuart, *One Hundred Years on Biscayne Bay 1887-1987*, Biscayne Bay Yacht Club, 1987.

Miami City Directory, R. L. Polk & Co., 1904, 1908, 1911, 1914, 1916, 1920, 1921, 1924, 1927, 1929, 1930, 1932, 1934, 1940, 1957, 1967, 1973.

Norton, Charles, *A Handbook of Florida*, Longmans, Green, & Co., New York, 1892.

Parkinson, C. Northcote, *Parkinson's Law*, Ballantine Books, New York, 1957.

Parks, Arva Moore, *Miami the Magic City*, Walsworth Press, Marceline, 1991.

Ibid, Miami Memoirs by John Sewell, A New Pictorial Edition, Arva Parks & Co., Miami, 1987.

Peters, Virginia Bergman, *The Florida Wars*, Archon Books, 1979.

Peters, Thelma, *Miami 1909*, Banyan Books, Inc., Miami, 1984.

Tebeau, Charlton W., *A History of Florida*, University of Miami Press, Coral Gables, Florida, 1971.

Tiger, Stephen, *The Miccosukees*, Miami—The Sophisticated Tropics, by Morton Beebe, Chronical Books, San Francisco, 1991.

Townshend, Frederick Trench, *Wildlife in Florida with a visit to Cuba*, Hurst and Blackett, London, c1875.

Williams, John Lee,*The Territory of Floridas*, A.T. Goodrich, New York, 1837.

Journals & Magazines

Ammidown, Margot, *The Wagner Family: Pioneer Life on the Miami River*, Tequesta 1982, Historical Association of Southern Florida, Miami.

Bentley, George R., *Colonel Thompson's "Tour of Tropical Florida,"* Tequesta 1950, Historical Association of Southern Florida, Miami.

Black, Hugo L., Jr., *Richard Fitzpatrick's South Florida, 1822-1840*, Tequesta 1980 & 1981, Historical Association of Southern Florida, Miami.

Buchanan, Patricia (Mrs. James), *Miami's Bootleg Boom*, Tequesta 1970, Historical Association of Southern Florida, Miami; and Master's Thesis, University of Miami, 1968.

Burkhardt, H. J., *Starch Making: A Pioneer Florida Industry*, Tequesta 1952, Historical Association of Southern Florida, Miami.

Carr, Robert, *The Brickell Store and Seminole Indian Trade*, Florida Anthropologist, Vol. 34, No. 4, December 1981.

Davis, T. Frederick, *Juan Ponce de Leon's Voyages to Florida*, Florida Historical Quarterly, April 1968.

Downs, Dorothy, *Coppinger's Tropical Gardens: The First Commercial Indian Village in Florida*, Florida Anthropologist, Vol. 34, No. 4, December 1981.

Gaby, Donald C., *A Rundown on South Florida Storms*, Update, Historical Association of of Southern Florida, May 1986.

Ibid., *The Early Years Upriver*, Tequesta 1988, Historical Association of Southern Florida, Miami.

Ibid., *What Would it Cost Today?*, South Florida History Magazine, Winter 1991 (also Spring & Summer 1989), Historical Association of Southern Florida, Miami.

Ibid., *The Curtiss Flying School and U.S. Marine Flying Field*, South Florida History Magazine, Summer 1991, Historical Association of Southern Florida, Miami.

Goggin, J. M., *The Tequesta Indians of Southern Florida*, Florida Historical Quarterly, Vol. 18, 1940.

Hudson, F. M., *Beginnings in Dade County*, Tequesta 1943, Historical Association of Southern Florida, Miami.

MacGonigle, The Rev. John N., *The Geography of the Southern Peninsula of the United States*, National Geographic Magazine, Washington, December 1896.

Marchman, W. P., *The Ingraham Everglades Exploring Expedition, 1892*, Tequesta 1947, Historical Association of Southern Florida, Miami.

McNicoll, Robert E., *The Caloosa Village Tequesta: A Miami of the Sixteenth Century*, Tequesta 1941, Historical Association of Southern Florida, Miami.

Parks, Arva Moore, *Miami in 1876*, Tequesta 1975, Historical Association of Southern Florida, Miami.

Shappee, Nathan D.,*Flagler's Undertaking in Miami in 1897*, Tequesta 1959, Historical Association of Southern Florida, Miami.

Ibid., *Fort Dallas and the Naval Depot on Key Biscayne, 1836-1926*, Tequesta 1961, Historical Association of Southern Florida, Miami.

Wagner, Henry, J. *Early Pioneers of South Florida* , Tequesta 1949, Historical Association of Southern Florida, Miami.

West, Patsy, *The Miami Indian Tourist Attractions*, Florida Anthropologist, Vol. 34, No. 4, December 1981.

Government Publications

City Manager's Report to City Commission of Five Years of Commission Manager Government for the City of Miami, 1926.

Congressional Report 242, No. 47, pp.10-38, 30th Congress, 1848.

Griffin, John W., Carl D. Murray, et al, *Excavations at the Granada Site*, Archaeology and History of the Granada Site, Volume I, Florida Division of Archives, History, and Records Management, Tallahassee, 1984.

House Document No. 295, 54th Congress, 2nd session, *Survey of Biscayne Bay*, 15 February 1897.

House Document, No. 662, 56th Congress, 1st session, 1900.

Ives, J. C., *Memoir to Accompany a Military Map of the Peninsula of Florida, South of Tampa Bay*, 1856, U.S. National Archives.

Leach, S. D., and R. G. Grantham, *Salt-Water Study of the Miami River and it Tributaries, Dade County, Florida*, Florida Geological Survey Report of Investigations 45, 1966.

Minutes of the Florida Internal Improvement Fund (trustees), 1909-1936, Florida State Archives, Tallahassee.

Parker, Garard G., et al, *Water Resources of Southeastern Florida*. With Special Reference to the Geology and Ground Water of the Miami Area, Geological Survey Water-Supply Paper 1225, U.S. Government Printing Office, Washington, 1955.

Parks, Arva Moore, *Where the River Found the Bay*, Volume 2, Archaeology and History of the Granada Site, Florida Division of Archives, History, and Records Management, Tallahassee, 1984.

Planning Study of the Miami River, Metropolitan Dade County Planning Department, Miami, April 1962.

Report of the Florida Everglades Engineering Commission to the Board of Commissioners of the Everglades Drainage District, State of Florida, 1913.

Reports of the Chief of Engineers, U.S. Army, 1909-1914 and 1930-1933, Jacksonville District Office, Florida and Defence Department Library, Washington.

Senate Document No. 5, 31st Congress, 1st session, 1850.

Senate Document No. 89, 62nd Congress, 1st session, serial 6108, 1911.

Smith, Hugh M., *Notes on Biscayne Bay*, Government Printing Office, Washington, 1896.

Newspapers

The Miami Metropolis, 1896-1923.

The Miami News-Metropolis, 1923-1924.

Miami Daily News, 1924-1925, 1932-38.

The Miami Evening Record, 1903-1907.

Miami Morning News-Record, 1908-1910.

The Miami Herald, 1911-1925, 1927-1931.

Miami Tribune, 1924-1927.

Illustrated Daily Tab, 1925.

Other Sources

George, Paul Sargis, *Criminal Justice in Miami: 1896-1930*, thesis, Florida State University, Tallahassee, 1975.

Grutzbach, Mrs. Margaret Rogers, personal communications, written and oral, with the author re early Miami and its waters.

Hempstead, Weston Franklin, Sr., *Record*, a personal record maintained from January 1924 through 1935, loaned to the author by Wes. Hempstead, Jr., 1986.

Jones, Cleveland H., Jr., interview and various conversations with the author, 1986 to 1991.

Newman, Thomas W., interview with the author, 1992.

Parks, Arva Moore, Notes from an unpublished manuscript by Arva M. Parks, 1987.

Ibid., Notes from her Biscayne Bay file, loaned, 1987.

Ibid., Arva Moore, Notes from set of cards regarding the Miami River prepared by Prof. Charlton W. Tebeau, loaned, 1987.

Public Records of Dade County, Florida.

Richards, Rose Wagner, *"Reminiscences of the Early Days of Miami,"* A series, Miami News, 1903. (See Agnew Welsh Notebook XXXVI, Miami-Dade Public Library.)

Shaw, Mrs. Mary Hodsdon, interview with the author, 1987.

Thomson, C. Eliot, Sr., *The Story of Miami Shipbuilding Corporation*, Historical Association of Southern Florida, Miami, plus interview with Jean E. Buhler, 1986.

Maps

1845: Survey of Southeast Florida, by George McKay, deputy surveyor, State of Florida, 1845.

1849: The mouth of the Miami River, by F. H. Gerdes, U.S. surveyor, Senate Document No. 5, 31st Congress, 1850.

1850: Map of the area of Biscayne Bay, by an officer stationed at Fort Dallas during the Second Seminole War, page 15, *Miami–The Way We Were.* by Howard Kleinberg, Miami Daily News, Inc., Miami, 1985.

1855: Map of the area of Biscayne Bay and the Miami River by Lt. I. M. Robertson, U.S. Army, RG-393, M1090 (10-35-2), National Archives, Washington. (This appears to be the same map as above, perhaps drawn from memory.)

1856: Military Map of Florida south of Tampa Bay, Lt. J. C. Ives, Topographical Engineer, by Order of Jefferson Davis, Secretary of War, Florida State Archives.

1896: The Mouth of the Miami River, Biscayne Bay, Florida, by Lt. Col. W. H. Benyaurd, Corps of Engineers, U.S. Army, P. K. Yonge Library, University of Florida, Gainesville.

1899, 1906, 1910, 1914, 1916, 1921, 1928, 1938, 1940, 1951: Insurance Maps of Miami, Florida; Sanborn Map Co., New York, University of Florida Maps Library, Gainesville.

1905, 1920, 1943: Official maps of the City of Miami, Florida, Historical Museum of Southern Florida, Miami.

1913, 1914, 1917: State of Florida surveys of the Miami River and Miami Canal, Florida Department of Natural Resources, Tallahassee.

1932, March (before dredging) and November 1934 (after dredging): U.S. Army Corps of Engineers surveys of the Miami River and Canal, District Office, Jacksonville, Florida.

1962, photo revised 1969: U.S. Geological Survey 7.5 minute series (topographic) map, Miami Quadrangle.

1974: Official map of the City of Miami, Florida; City of Miami Survey Office, Miami.

Index

About the Author

Author Donald C. Gaby

Donald C. Gaby is a retired satellite meteorologist turned amateur historian. His first knowledge of the river came on frequent visits to downtown Miami as a boy in the late 1930s and early 1940s. He first became interested in the history of the Miami River after purchasing a home on the Miami Canal, just above where it joins the Miami River and only a few blocks from the former rapids at the edge of the Everglades. He lived with his wife on the Miami Canal for 12 years before they moved about one mile downstream to an apartment overlooking the Miami River itself. Thus, he has lived on the Miami River "system" for some 14 years, and he hopes for many more.

Don Gaby's first book-length publication on the Miami River, *An Historical Guide to the Miami River and Its Tributaries*, was published in 1990 by the Historical Association of Southern Florida as a portable pocket guide. After many favorable comments and inquiries, the institution has published this comprehensive work that more completely reflects Gaby's research and depth of knowledge. He also shared his expertise on the river in 1988 as guest curator for the Historical Museum's full-scale exhibition on the Miami River.

Don Gaby's research has taken him to the National Archives, the Library of Congress, Defense Department Library, Florida Department of Natural Resources, Florida State Archives, Historical Museum of Southern Florida, Dade County Public Records Library, university libraries and public libraries. Much information has been gathered by reading the early Miami newspapers, and by talking with persons who lived in Miami much earlier. He has tended to concentrate on the early history where it is available, and to leave later periods for a comprehensive second edition or another historian. The author likes to think that his early scientific training is well suited to historical research—both fields of endeavor being concerned with seeking the truth, however it may be found.